Folk Songs
of
Old Hampshire

Edited and described by
JOHN PADDY BROWNE

MILESTONE PUBLICATIONS

Published by
Milestone Publications
62 Murray Road,
Horndean, Hampshire PO8 9JL

Design Brian Iles
Cover design Helen Berners
Cover photograph John J. Philpott, ARPS

Typeset by Barbara James, Hayling Island, Hants
Printed and bound in Great Britain by
R.J. Acford, Industrial Estate, Chichester, Sussex

British Library Cataloguing in Publication Data

Hampshire folk songs.
  1. Folk-songs, English——England——
Hampshire
  I. Browne, John Paddy
  784.4'94227   M1740

  ISBN 1-85265-106-7

By the same author:
Selected Poems
Map Cover Art

For Nathaniel Joseph

Contents

Acknowledgements

My thanks to the English Folk Dance and Song Society for permission to use songs from the George B. Gardiner collection; to Frank Purslow for song arrangements from the Gardiner collection, edited by him for his books *Marrow Bones* and *The Constant Lovers*; to Bob Copper for two songs collected by him and preserved in the Copper family's repertoire; to Terry Gregory for the broadside *The Southampton Tragedy* in his collection; to Graham Penny, Brian Hooper, Ken Stephens and Michael Sadler for original songs written by them; to the Prison Reform Society for information; to John Foreman (The Broadsheet King) for the information in his reproductions of early song books; and to Andy Howes who, as my amanuensis, has had to listen to me singing these songs or has had to decipher my incognizable notes. Any errors in the musical transcriptions can only be blamed on my shortcomings as singer and scrivener.

Bill Eddie typeset the musical notations, and Sue Crossley set chords to the tunes.

I have tried to locate the copyright owners of all the material used in this book, including the illustrations; if I have failed to contact you all, it was not for want of trying and I do apologise.

Hampshire

The County takes its name from Southampton and used to be called Southamptonshire. The Romans, led by Laelius Hamo, had accepted surrender from the British chief Guiderius, but when they killed Guiderius, the chief's brother killed Hamo. The spot where Hamo was killed was from that day known as *Hamos Town* or Hampton. In time the named evolved into Hamptonshire. . .

So the story goes.

Hampshire folk songs are every bit as colourful.

Foreword

I have taken a few liberties with the meaning of the term 'folk song' in this book. Everyone has his or her own idea of what a folk song is. The nature of folk song has, as we shall see, never been satisfactorily defined, even by so-called experts, although a great deal of time and energy has been expended in the attempt.

Not all the songs in this book are folk songs in the sense of the term as we know it, but all of them possess many of the qualities of folk song. If, for example, anonymity is a prerequisite of the folk song, then some of these songs are not folk songs because we know who made them. If antiquity is a prerequisite, then others are not folk songs because, while we may not know who wrote them, they are not very old. And so on. But all the songs in this collection deserve their place here because they mirror a common life and speak for our community — and that is an absolute necessity if any song is to qualify for the label 'folk song'.

Added to that is the fact that all the songs here are eminently singable, and no song can be called a folk song if the 'folk' can't sing it.

I have selected songs which have a bearing on the old county of Hampshire and the Isle of Wight — that is, the county which existed before the Local Government Act of 1972 robbed the county of the Island, Bournemouth and Poole and some other territory. This is relevant only insofar as that some of these songs were collected on the borders of the old county and might now be claimed by enthusiastic plagairists as 'Dorset' songs or 'West Sussex' songs when they are patently nothing of the sort. Those counties have enough songs of their own.

The collection may be divided into two broad categories: songs directly *about* Hampshire and songs collected in Hampshire which may exist elsewhere. The urge to include the latter, sometimes at the expense of the former, was irresistible for one reason or another, and I have tried to explain my criteria for selection in the descriptive notes which accompany each song.

Folk songs do not sit well on the five-line musical stave — what A.L. Lloyd called 'piano-tuner's music'. This stave is too restrictive to capture the embellishments of the folk singer's vocal line, or the improvisations which he made to the metre. Bartók, collecting folk songs and trying to commit them to the printed page, used tiny arrows above the notes to indicate whether these notes should be sung a little above or below the stave line.

Few folk songs have verses of equal metric or syllabic value, and so it is impossible to represent the whole song with one verse under the tune. The singer must use his or her common sense and lose a little inhibition when singing these songs. I refuse to straightjacket the songs any further by giving musical notations for every verse.

John Paddy Browne

'Three yards a penny! Three yards a penny! Beautiful songs! Newest songs! Popular songs! Three yards a penny!
It is doubtful whether many of the songs in this ballad-monger's budget would have been 'beautiful', but many would have been popular, especially if they dealt with local scandals, great sea victories, rapes, murders or executions.

Introduction

If the songs of Hampshire lack the drama of the great ballads of Scotland and the border regions and the vitality of the industrial songs of the northern mines and mills, they are not without a quality of their own. It is true that, although Hampshire is a county which boasts two sea-ports — one a major passenger port, the other an important naval port — the sea songs are not in the same class as the great shanties of the country's ocean-going traders. These shanties were the product of the mighty Liverpool and Bristol, New York, Baltimore, Nova Scotia, Newfoundland and Philadelphia clipper ships, engaged against each other in a fierce struggle for mercantile supremacy of the Atlantic in the mid-to-late 19th century. From this period come England's most vigorous songs. Shanties were working songs, used by the masters and crew of the merchant navy to help streamline such chores as pushing capstans, hauling sails, dragging ropes, and so on. The Royal Navy, used to working to orders, had no use and no place for shanties; their songs tend to be about battles and commanders.

Nor can Hampshire lay claim to ballads of the quality of the epic tales which dominate Scottish and north-east English folklore, even though Hampshire has seen great fleets and great armies set out for immortality at Trafalgar and Agincourt and Waterloo. The massacre of a church-full of Southampton's citizens by French pirates on Sunday October 4, 1338, near the outbreak of the 'Hundred Year War' with France, went virtually unnoticed by the balladmakers of the day. Had this disaster taken place in Scotland we would have had a dozen hour-long ballads about it.

Hampshire's folk songs rather resemble the county's topography: they roll gently. Just as the Turneresque bleakness of Scotland's highlands suit the epic ballads and the 'dark Satanic mills' of the English north and midlands are stamped on the country's industrial songs, so the lush landscapes of the south undulate harmoniously throughout the south's folk songs.

There are exceptions everywhere, of course. There are gentle love songs among the murderous Scottish epics and the grimy, gritty industrial songs; there are wistfully nostalgic sea songs (known to sailors as *forebitters* or *fo'c'sle songs*) in the midst of the hardnosed shanties; and there are belligerent war songs in the soft folds of the Hampshire downs.

Hampshire has been the stage for many events of outstanding historical significance. The wealth of prehistoric remains in the county bears witness to the activities of a highly-cultivated early man. The natural facilities of the county's sheltered waterways attracted Roman attention and drew in early seafaring traders. Our proximity to the continent of Europe has given us cause for anxiety on many occasions, and we can still find relics of that anxiety in the ruins of iron-age hill forts, anti-Napoleon pill boxes, and old airfields from which Hampshire-built Spitfires set out to defeat the arch tyrant.

Town walls still stand to remind us of an age-old fear of invasion; and if we listen carefully to our thoughts as we stand under the arch of an ancient bargate, we might still hear the tramp of soldiers on their way to put the French or the Spaniards or the Germans in their place. We can, should we so wish, look at half-demolished churches and monasteries and nunneries and remember a time when Englishman fought Englishman, and a king lost his head.

All of these images of the past come echoing back to us in our folk songs. But folk songs are not only concerned with important historical events.

Nelson's victory at Trafalgar might have been an ideal subject for a folk song, but so, too, was the smashing of some machinery by anxious labourers on a farm in remote Owslebury. And so, too, was the murder of a little girl in a field at Alton. And so, too, was the courtship between dozens of lovelorn couples, plighting their troths in countless moonlit nights, often against the wishes of cruel, misunderstanding parents. No subject is too big or too trivial for a folk song.

So what is a folk song?

I once put this question to A.L. Lloyd, one of this country's most knowledgeable folk song collectors and author of a definitive book on the subject. He shrugged his shoulders and said, 'What *is* a folk song?', which was a great help.

But there is more perplexity in that reply than you might imagine. Until Lloyd wrote his book *Folk Song in England* in 1967, the only really serious attempt at a definition was Cecil Sharp's *English Folk Song: Some Conclusions*, published in 1907. Sharp remained unchallenged for six decades, but his conclusions *should* have been challenged long before that, if only because his ideas of what folk song was all about were evolved through his study of the songs from — in the main — a very small area of England, and a rural, idyllic part of England at that: a couple of small villages in Somerset. He closed his mind to any concept of folk song which did not fit the stereotype of the folk singer as a sort of Noble Savage, a romantic illiterate in possession of an emotional impulse which could create a pure folk song out of thin air and who, in addition to this wondrous facility, held a repertoire of similarly pure traditional songs in his head. Sharp chose to ignore the rising wave of industrial songs largely because industrial song was being created out of an increasing literacy, as the effects of the new national educational systems began to take effect. To Sharp, education spelled out the end of the emotional impulse in the common man, and with it the end of folk song as an evolving, living organism.

The singers encountered by Sharp in his perambulations of Somerset's country byways offered him more than folk songs: they offered him the popular 'commercial' songs of the day, music hall songs, and sometimes lewd but quite genuine folk songs. But this was not what Sharp wanted to hear and he refused to record it. It upset his notion of the English folk singer as Noble Savage. Discarding the kaleidoscopic repertoire of the true traditional singer, Sharp presented his singers as an idyll, as carriers of an untarnished tradition, singing songs of an England which never existed and never could exist. His *Conclusions* were further restricted by the fact that, from the small area of Somerset in which he worked, he chose only selected songs from a very few inhabitants. As a result, *Conclusions* is hardly a representative report on the folk songs of Somerset much less an authoritative analysis of English folk song as a whole.

Sharp wasn't alone in this notion of the English folk song and its singer: the age in which he lived, a restrictive and oppressive age, influenced even the most liberal academic. Certainly literature was tightly controlled and books were a strongly-harnessed medium of communication. If Sharp finally managed to overcome his qualms about his singers' repertoires and take down in his notebooks an accurate rendering of the songs they gave him, what he was able to publish subsequently fell far short of the true nature of English folk song. Throughout Sharp's published song books we find versions of English folk songs which are meaningless because the symbolism which graces most folk cultures — a sometimes overt symbolism — has been distorted or excised completely, and the essential spirit of the songs has been killed off. In many cases the songs have, if you like, been rendered gutless and bowdlerised beyond recognition. A song such as *The Keys of Heaven* which we know to be a song of explicit amorous metaphor becomes a coy litany of nonsensical images in the published versions. Nobody encountering the song for the first time in a book will have the vaguest idea of its meaning: hearing it on the lips of a traditional singer requires no explanations.

In Hampshire, the great folk song collector was George Balfour Gardiner, a Scottish academic who, in 1905, undertook to gather up the surviving folk songs of the county at the behest of the then Folk Song Society. Gardiner, with only six years left to live, collected an astonishing 1500 songs from the workhouses, farms, pubs and fairs of the county. His collection is one of the major sources for folk song study in Britain, although Gardiner, in common with Sharp and the other collectors of the day, was selective in his published texts. Some doubtful items, however, managed to slip through the net and songs like *Jim the Carter Lad* which owe more to the stage countryman of the music hall than to the worker in the fields, have found their way into serious collections, often on account of beguiling performances by old singers of the likes of George Belton from Sussex, a once frequent visitor to Hampshire folk clubs and festivals.

It is unlikely that the 'true' folk singer was sufficiently adept at recognising the music hall trespasser in his repertoire to be able to refine his material to suit the notions and preconceptions of the early collectors. Far from possessing an emotional impulse only (or what the poet Edwin Muir called a 'lyric impulse') to create pure folk songs, the traditional singer more than likely possessed an emotional *response* to certain songs, tunes or lyrics, and these songs could be a mish-mash of many cultures and many traditions. Hence we find sentimental songs like *Silver Threads Among the Gold* and true folk songs like *The Seeds of Love* in the same singer's songbag, and songs of Irish origin flowing quite happily from the lips of an English country singer *vide* Mrs Munday's redition of *The Croppy Boy* to Gardiner at Axford, Basingstoke, in 1907. This phenomenon, this interbreeding of folk song cultures, is not exclusively English: in this book you will find songs which have swopped traditions from one country or another, and we have examples of songs which have adapted themselves so successfully to another tradition as to be almost unrecognisable. Such is the case of the Irish song *The Star of the County Down* which has stolen the tune from the English ballad *Dives and Lazarus*. There are many similar instances of tradition interchanges.

The Ballads
There are few narrative ballads which are native to the south of England and, despite the importance of some of our historical events, fewer still of distinct relevance to Hampshire. The tradition of ballad-making seems to have entered Britain with the arrival of the Vikings in the 9th century AD, and most of the grander ballads certainly carry on a spirit which we can only loosely and unsatisfactorily describe as 'Nordic'. By this I mean that the ballads concern themselves with events of heroic scale: the dissolution of clans and tribes; the political intrigues of feudal chiefs; great battles between kings and pretenders; their murders, their heroic deeds, and their failures. The broad sweep of the balladic canvas is of a spectacular landscape.

The British ballad tradition developed most forcefully in Scotland and in the north-east corners of England, and there is a regional sub-culture known as 'the Border Ballads' centred on the counties which sit astride the boundary between the two countries. Not all ballads, however, are of great events: but even in recording relatively minor occurrences there is a certain ballad *form* which seeks to tell a story. At its most dilute, this ballad form may be found in the so-called *Come-all-ye* songs, a *genre* which overspills with an extravagant language at its most elegiac. This can be utterly charming, but it reaches a nadir in the hack writings of the broadside peddlars, of which more presently.

Despite the importance of historical events in our own county, from the arrival of the Romans right up to the massive assemblies of armies preparing for the D-Day landings of the Second World War, few ballad writers or ballad makers rose to tell the tale, and thus our history was left to the writers of history books. The Royal Navy at Portsmouth fared somewhat better, but even then many of the songs relating to events taking place in or from Portsmouth were of the unremarkable broadside calibre and very few lived on in the folk song tradition. John Ashton's famous book *Real Sailor Songs*, which carried a good many Hampshire-related ballads and songs, failed to secure any premanence for his songs in the folk singer's repertoire: the absence of tunes from his book didn't help.

As it happens, any ballads which do exist in Hampshire tend to be strays from Scotland and the north-east, brought south by itinerant ballad mongers and singers, and later on by printed song sheets and broadsides. Thus our *Outlandish Knight* has no relevance to Hampshire other than that it has been found to exist here, nestling side by side in the mind of my Lymington singer with songs of a more parochial significance. The main interest of all this is that a narrative ballad has managed to survive into the twentieth century, having lived for a couple of hundred years on the lips of traditional folk singers interested enough in the ballad to keep passing it on from one generation to the next. When we discover a song in this way, especially one so anachronistically misplaced as a northern ballad in a south-coast country town, we are always tempted to say that we have saved it from extinction at the last moment; that our singer would probably have been the last person to keep the song alive; that this one example was the epitome of all folk songs — they were all on the brink of extinction.

Sharp believed this to be the case, and all collectors since his day have warned that English folk song is, indeed, in its death throes. Yet collectors in the late 1980's are still uncovering hordes of long-lost folk songs, and among them there are a good number of ballads. When I recently travelled to a remote country region to make a television film on folk song collecting, I discovered that the visit of our film unit had been enshrined in a ballad made up by the village ballad-maker! Far from television accelerating the demise of folk song creation, television became part of the writer's fodder. Unselfconscious, spontaneous and quite objective, the little ballad about our visit was in true come-all-ye style and could sit quite happily with all other songs in the *genre*.

The urge to write ballads, be they about great events or about trivial, domestic situations, may be a lyric impulse; or it may simply be the common man giving air to occurrences which arrest his attention or tickle his fancy. The form is already there, predestined; the language is that carried down the ages to him; anonymity will creep over his work in due course as his song goes on its way and he slips into the background. A new folk song will have been created, and those who tell us that folk song and the facility for inventing a new ballad on a subject are lost arts will be dumbfounded.

It fell to an American professor, Francis J. Child, to compile the most formidable collection of ballads, together with all their known variants, ever — or since — published. This mighty five-volume work comes complete with an essay on the history and development of the British ballad, confirming the associations between British traditions and those of European countries. *The English and Scottish Popular Ballads* was published between 1882 and 1898 and remains majestically impressive after all these years. Flawed in only one respect, Child failed to give the tunes for most of the entries in his collection, and this shortcoming was not put right until the middle part of this century when another American professor, Bertrand Bronson, began to publish his equally impressive tome, *The Traditional Tunes of the Child Ballads*.

There had existed other collections of ballads before Child: John Selden (1584-1654) provided the nucleus of what was to become the Samuel Pepys ballads, one of the most impressive collections anywhere in the world; and Anthony Wood (1632-1695) made a collection which was pilfered by — among others — the first Earl of Oxford and the third Duke of Roxburghe. Bishop Percy (1729-1811) caught a servant lighting a fire with a bundle of papers which turned out to be a massive collection of old ballads. Percy gathered the remnants together, continued to add further ballads to the collection and subsequently published his still-famous *Reliques of Ancient English Poetry*, nowadays known to folk song students as *Percy's Reliques*.

Sir Walter Scott published his *Border Minstrelsy* between 1802 and 1803; still available in various reprints and facsimile editions, Scott's *Minstrelsy* is a landmark in folk song scholarship and a much-used reference book.

Then, just before Child, there appeared the 9-volume *Roxburghe Ballads*, the last of the truly great collections. None of these impressive works stood up against the astonishing scholarship brought to British balladry by Child, and to this day we refer to ballads covered by the Child collection as 'Child 234' or 'Child 79', or whatever.

The broadsides
Professor Child had few kind words for the broadside ballads, dismissing them as 'veritable dunghills in the midst of which only the occasional moderate jewel may be found'. We can see what he meant as we plough our way through the huge collections of the usually trash verses — the forerunners of today's tabloid newspapers.

Long before the tabloid newspapers and the broadside ballads, and long before Caxton's printing press, folk song was handed down from singer to singer, generation to generation, in a cycle which we call 'oral transmission' — the passing on by word of mouth. Folk song both suffered from this process and benefitted by it. It suffered in that the diffusion of a song by an increasing number of singers gradually whittled away those parts of the song which did not appeal to the singer, or it took on bits of other songs which *did* appeal to him. Much in the same way that a story told by one person to another changes as person B passes it on to person C and so on, so folk songs have changed as they passed from one singer to another. In addition to this, songs changed as they drifted from one district to another and became adapted to the needs of their new location. Thus, a song which once began with the words 'As I was going to Portsmouth...' might become 'As I was going to Salisbury...' even though the gist of the story remained intact, or more or less so.

Singers were adept at salvaging fragments of other songs in order to patch up incomplete versions of songs which they wished to sing. These fragments have become known as 'floating verses', for they float between different songs and reappear in many forms. The well-known *Love is teasing and love is pleasing/And love is a pleasure when first it's new/But as it grows older so love grows colder/And fades away like the morning dew* is a widespread floating verse which has

Broadside ballads were often sold in the streets and at fairs and market places. This woodcut shows a 17th century hawker holding up what appears to be a gothic 'black letter' song sheet complete with illustration.

attached itself to a great number of songs, as well as being a song in its own right.

At the same time, all this helped to make some uninteresting songs a little more attractive, and very often a mediocre folk song has been improved by the acquisition of a floating verse. Regional variations developed in the oral transmission process often improved tired old songs and gave them a new lease of life. In some cases, the original words have disappeared and all we are left with are songs which are almost wholly constructed of floating verses. Such a song is *I Wish, I Wish, but all in Vain/I wish I was a maid again/But that's one thing I cannot be/Till apples grow on an orange tree*: the whole song is made up of fragments of other songs, including *Love is Teasing*.

This process of oral transmission degenerated with the development of the broadside ballad and the later introduction of education for the working classes; a social change which fossilised the traditional folk song, whether lyric or ballad, whether local or national, and inhibited its development as an evolving, ever-changing song form. Once songs were written down they tended not to change so much as they would have done when passed from mouth to mouth; when they were printed on widely-circulated song sheets or 'chapbooks' the chances of development were unlikely to be very great. We are told of people buying broadsides and penny song sheets from door-to-door sellers and from market place singers, taking the sheets home and pinning them to the parlour wall by which means they might easily be learned. Thus the printed song became 'frozen' in form and feature, and this was essentially the fate of the broadside ballad.

So what were these broadside ballads? Where did they come from? What did they concern themselves with? And are there any of relevance to old Hampshire?

To put the cart before the horse, the answer to the last question is a loud 'Yes': there are a great many broadside ballads relating to Hampshire, and several are to be found in this book.

Broadside ballads were, in the words of Gershon Legman, 'the combined murder mysteries and comic books of their time'. They might have changed in appearance as the years went by, moving from heavy-handed gothic black letter type to clumsily printed sheets on flimsy paper, with an astonishing number of mis-spellings in the text, and with the gory woodcut illustrations sometimes even printed the wrong way up. Finesse, whether in style or substance, was not the concern of the broadside which existed to get hard news and comment out on the market place as quickly as possible. The literary hacks who churned out this material rode roughshod over such matters as grammar, poetic refinement, and the susceptibilities of the squeamish. With all the restraint of today's Sunday tabloids, they gloried in sensationalism, moralised in the most grotesque manner on the misfortunes of the hapless, and maintained a lofty hypocrisy which, generally speaking, justified Professor Child's dismissal of the *genre*.

In the mid-16th century, broadside printers were required by law to register their products with the Stationers' Company and, although not all publishers did so, recent scholars have located more than three thousand entries for the first 150 years. A large part of the Pepys collection, which we have already touched on, comprised contemporary broadsides, and some broadsides (Child's 'occasional moderate jewels') did, in fact, appeal to the more refined tastes of the political satirist or the bourgeois versifier.

The first broadsides are probably those dealing with Robin Hood's exploits and date from about 1490, according to William Chappell in his marathon study of English song, *Popular Music of the Olden Time*, published in two hefty volumes in 1859. With the rise of newspapers, the 'news' content of the broadside began to change emphasis, and the more able readers of the populace turned away from the gutter style of the broadside in favour of the new medium, especially in the search for details about foreign events such as wars and political activities. The broadside turned in upon itself and, again in common with the more lurid modern tabloids, dealt more and more with the darker corners of humankind.

Folk songs, and new songs in a folk idiom, arose in popularity with the broadside-buying public and, in the families of broadside printers, empires began to be built. James Catnach of London's Moorfields, Henry Such of the Borough, and Mother Pitts of Portsmouth, who moved to Seven Dials in London to create the Pitts family printers, vied with each other for supremacy. Sales were enormous: one printer had over five thousand different texts in his catalogue and another sold more than a million-and-a-half copies of the Maria Marten Red Barn murder. The more sensational the event being recorded, the larger would be the print run and the wider the sales. Thus murders were perfect fodder for the broadside printer, and executions were especially lucrative. At least four different broadsides were available in Winchester on the morning of Christmas Eve 1867 when Frederick Baker was hanged before a large crowd for the murder of Fanny Adams. The poignancy of the date, its close proximity to a day traditionally held by Christians to be one of peace and happiness, appears to have been completely lost on the printers (as well, apparently, as on the crowd of spectators) who moralised on the events which led to this unhappy state of affairs. These four broadsides, all by different printers, all tell somewhat different stories (one even gets the date of the murder wrong by three days), and all adopt different stances; but they all bear the unmistakable stamp of the tabloid's hypocritical moral tone, denouncing the violence of the crime while at the same time glorying morbidly in its details. The report in the *Illustrated Police News*, a journal of unimaginable turpitude, leaves no gruesome detail to the imagination and even carries two crude drawings of the unfortunate Fanny Adams being lured to her death, and her slayer, Baker, holding up the severed head.

When the nation's gallows were not in operation (which seems to have been not very often), the broadside printer turned his attention to other items: scandals, the doings of Royalty, the comings and goings of merchant ships, battles, political intrigues, celebrity courtships — or even the courtships of unknown local couples — freaks of nature, religious tracts or parodies of them such as *The Soldier's Catechism*, — or good old folk songs. Folk songs occupied a relatively large part of the broadside balladeer's stock in trade and a great many of the songs we are now able to study have come down to us in printed versions. One could argue that, when the lifespan of many a folk song had run its course on the lips of the traditional singer passing the song on in the oral transmission process, it was saved from extinction by being preserved in print. For this reason, if for no other, we have cause to be grateful to the broadside printer. One of our songs, *The Outlandish Knight*, might have lived on on the lips of traditional singers right down to the day I recorded it from a singer in Lymington; and, had I not found it when I did, it might well have been lost. However, it would not have been completely lost, for several versions of the ballad had already been printed and published as broadsides.

By the 19th century, the power of the broadside ballad began to wane in the south of England as the first arrivals of the reactionary middle class began to take the region out and above the breadline existence of the rest of the country. In 1811, Bournemouth existed only as the place where the tiny River Bourne entered the sea. However, the first villa which began the mass exodus to the south coast and the creation of the vast conurbation we know today, was about to be built, and the well-heeled population which swelled the new resort so swiftly and so spectacularly had little time for crudely printed song sheets. The great liner port of Southampton produced almost no broadsides relating to its most famous industry, although some sheets carried news or songs about other domestic events, such as the murder of Naomi Kingswell, a copy of which appears later in this book. If many more broadsides were printed, few of them have survived.

Portsmouth had the advantage of John Ashton's interest, for he collected a great number of naval broadsides for his handsome book *Real Sailor Songs* (1891), and several of these — or at least versions of them — turn up in our pages. Ashton reprinted the broadsides in the typefaces of his own day but retained, in most cases, the woodcuts which decorated the original sheets so that we can have an idea, at least, of what the ballads were like to look at.

The fortunes of the broadside ballad singer have ebbed and flowed as era succeeded era. In some communities the travelling songsmith was an honoured guest, able to pay for his supper with a new ballad on a theme, a paean to his host, or a comic song to set the table in good-natured uproar. But there were times, notably in the reign of the first Elizabeth, when the roving balladeer ran the risk of having an inch-wide hole burnt into his ear for peddling his wares; if he didn't learn by that lesson, a third conviction took him to the gallows where he himself might end up the subject of one of his compatriot's verses. In Victorian times, London policemen were not unknown to draw truncheons in order to disperse ballad singers hawking their chapbooks and penny song-sheets around the far-famed Ratcliffe highway.

In due course 'legitimate' songbooks appeared, carrying verses and pretty tunes more in keeping with the drawing room than the farmhouse or the spit-and-sawdust or the street corner. Generally known as 'garlands', these attractive little books occasionally carried quite authentic folk songs and, it is conceivable that in some quarters, folk songs attained a certain respectability so long as their themes and sentiments offered no threat to the establishment *status quo*. Curiously, there were some phenomenal aberrations spawned in the midst of all this, few more remarkable than the case of the Irish song-writer, Thomas Moore, whose songs *The Last Rose of Summer*, *The Minstrel Boy* and *Believe Me, if all Those Endearing Young Charms* are still world famous. Moore had seen his college mate, Robert Emmet, publicly hanged, drawn and quartered for his part in an ill-fated insurrection against English colonial rule in Ireland. The singing of rebellious folk songs was prohibited at this time in Ireland (as it is to some extent even today), but Moore wrote several songs lamenting his executed friend, some shrouded in a thin allegory, others dangerously overt. It is still a matter of astonishment to remember that Moore, who found great favour with the English upper classes ('Tommy loves a lord', wrote one contemporary critic disparagingly), could take these songs into the very homes of the people who had killed his friend and sing them to wild applause.

I mention this remarkable fact because it has a bearing on the status of the ballad singer in his own time and place, and also because Moore ended his days here in the south of England and is, in fact, buried under a splendid Celtic cross in the churchyard at Bromham, Wiltshire. His extensive diary shows how well he knew the county of Hampshire and, although his songs are beyond the scope of this book, several of his later ballads were written in this county.

One last element of the broadside ballad is worth reflecting upon: while some of these sheets carried tunes, most echoed the universal musical illiteracy of the working classes and gave no melody lines. They made do with a byline which recommended that the words be sung to the tune of some popular song of the day. It was the last crude touch.

The Come-all-ye
Possibly the most persistently influential folk song type is that which we call the *Come-all-ye*. It rose to prominence in England with the arrival of vast numbers of improverished and disenfranchised Irish country dwellers leaving Ireland to escape the great famine which decimated that country in 1845 and the six years that followed. Simple in form, sometimes even simplistic, it was easy to make up and, because it appealed directly to the ear, it was easy to learn. Not many of these songs look very good on the printed page but in the mouth of a good lyrical singer they can have a potent effect. Their attraction is immediate and, at their best, they are indeed attractive songs.

They tend to follow an insistent pattern of four-lined strophes and an ABBA melody line which makes no demands on the listener beyond that of absorbing the message which the song carries. Although of a balladic content, albeit dealing with more domestic matters than the epic narratives, they lack the animal literacy of the 'big' ballads. They do, when they are so inclined, contain a literacy of their own which may or may not be deemed poetry. There is no doubt of the presence of a poetic mind in the shape and content of the come-all-ye and, if we consider the source of the come-all-ye, we will become aware of a deliberate literacy at work. The Irish come-all-ye, from which nearly all English variants derive, was the product of a class of people who were below the level of what we know in England as the working class. I say that because the people who constructed and evolved the form of the come-all-ye were the decendants of a race persecuted under the 'Penal Laws' imposed by a colonial occupying force; a government which prevented certain parts of the community from, for example, owning property worth more than £5, of having a house with more than two small windows, from practising their religion, and forming their own schools and educational systems, and so on.

These laws were quite emphatically enforced but, as with Hitler's bombing of Britain during the Second World War, far from crushing life out of the people, it merely hardened the people's resolve to stand up to it and to survive. One aspect of the Penal Laws in Ireland — one aspect of its effect on the people — was that it consolidated a need to 'improve' themselves, and, if not themselves as adults living under a foreign regime, then to give their children the means of improving *their* lot through the awareness of their religious traditions and by means of the best education possible under the circumstances.

This educational system, in post-Penal Law Ireland, took on a curious shape, and its effects are manifestly evident in the come-all-ye ballads. Because education to Roman Catholics was prohibited under the Laws, schoolmasters and itinerant pedagogues set up a network of so-called 'hedge schools' at which children and some adults were taught essential subjects, including basic classical languages. These hedge schools met in cottage parlours, barns, and — quite literally — behind hedges with sentries posted on hilltops to watch out for approaching redcoats.

The education itself had high aspirations even if it did not always attain what it aspired to. The languages interbred and the epic tales of Greece and Rome entwined inexorably with the native folklore. Aurora and Alexander met Cuchullain and Fionn MacCumhaill, and small villages took on the grandeur of heroic cities. All this found its way into the come-all-ye songs and in time these songs filtered across the sea to England (as well as America and Australia) and, in our own case, they have left their mark on the folk songs of old Hampshire, as we shall see.

The come-all-ye is so called because it often, but not exclusively, begins with that phrase. It may begin with other exhortations such as 'Attend again, brave comrades' or 'Come listen to my story...'; or the last verse, summing up the theme of the song and drawing a moral, may begin with one of these phrases. Their content is that of the domestic occurrence and this may include disasters at sea, failure of crops, executions and sensational murders, and — in England — coal pit tragedies and songs of seduction. The come-all-ye is available to everyone and it draws on all emotions.

In presenting its subject matter, the come-all-ye is often vague: in *Deep Sheephaven Bay*, the date of the fishing disaster is not revealed nor is any one of the lost crew named; in the English come-all-ye *Johnny Seddon*, the mine which collapses is not identified. Individuals in the community of come-all-ye scenarios are sometimes emblemished in a single mysterious figure such as the 'one who sits alone' mourning the tragedy of *Sheephaven Bay*, or the young woman who stands by a river, lamenting the losses in *Johnny Seddon* and — another mine disaster song — *The Blantyre Explosion*. In all cases, this mysterious figure represents the whole community: she is no one person: she is the universal weeping madonna, speaking for all.

When the come-all-ye attempts to record facts and figures it becomes notoriously unreliable. Numbers of people involved invariably increase and dates becomes nonsense. In this book you will find a song called *The Owslebury Lads*: all versions want to tell us that the events described in the song took place in 1813 when they did, in fact, take place in 1830. This is evidently a mis-hearing on the part of some early singer or ballad-printer who has set a chain sequence of errors in motion and carried the error right down to the present day. When I heard Turp Brown of Cheriton sing the song, he, too, sang 'eighteen thirteen'.

Local skirmishes between troublesome neighbours can often take on the proportions of a small war in the come-all-ye; and the 'tall tale' has found fertile soil in this malleable little art form. *Tally ho, Hark Away* , which we know from an Isle of Wight version, often ends up with the captured fox making a will in favour of his captors; similarly in *Larry's Goat*, the tormented creature

makes a will in which his least desirable parts are bequeathed to his
tormentors. This song begins with the lines 'Good people pay attention and
listen to my song. . .' and ends with another favoured theme of the come-all-ye:
the multiple curse by which a long litany of damnation is hurled at the head
of some unfortunate detractor, rather along these lines:

May his house never thatch, may his door never latch,
May his geese fly away like an old paper kite,
May his pigs never grunt, may his horse never hunt,
May a ghost ever haunt him at dead of the night. . .

Such, then, are the themes and style of the come-all-ye, the most common
of all our folk song types and the one which we are most likely to turn to if
we wish to write a song about some event quickly and entertainingly.

Later in this book, when I deal with the song *Gosport*, I write briefly about
some aspects of the come-all-ye, but perhaps at this point, we need to dwell a
little longer on this complex type of folk song. For the come-all-ye can be both
prosaic and sublime, matter-of-fact or puzzlingly obscure; it can pass over you
because of its sheer ordinariness or it can amaze by the dexterity of its style.
Content and subject matter have no control whatever over the style of
presentation in the come-all-ye. The most commonplace theme may find itself
spoken about in extravagant language and, conversely, exalted personages and
celebrated shrines may be dismissed with street-corner abruptness. Irony is a
favourite element of the *genre* , declamation a natural style, and outrageous
lyricism common enough. Frequently more than one of these elements are
combined to comic effect, and *Gosport* gives us a glimpse — but only a glimpse
— of this mixutre of elements.

At its lower levels, the come-all-ye gets on with a simple story, expressed in
a simple, no-frills style of language. The singer will be called upon to deliver
such a song in declamatory manner, without vocal ornamentation. On the
other hand, many of the great laments and many of folk song's great love songs
are composed within the framework of the come-all-ye, and so cleverly
contrived are they that it is with reluctance that we agree that they actually *are*
come-all-ye's, and not some grander song form.

Somewhere in between these poles, there lies the bulk of the come-all-ye with
its assonantic rhymes, its alliteration and flowery language, its plays on words,
its allusions to classical scholarship, its leg-pulling, and its sheer pathos. The
singer will rise to the occasion of such songs with an equally elaborate style
involving much lyrical decoration of the musical line and an extravagant vocal
delivery. He will make a great deal of the internal rhyming systems which
create rhymes out of assonances or straight matching words, and he will
elaborate on the humble theme dressed up in heroic disguise.

Such songs may sometimes have taxed the inventive powers of their creators
and certainly they reveal a considerable facility for scansion, rhyme and
cadence. After a while we begin to see a similarity of approach creeping in;
and after much study we are aware of a fairly rigid set of rules and patterns.
The fourteen syllables of the four-lined strophes, the 6/8 tunes, the familiar
insistence on half-line rhymes (as well as couplet rhymes on line ends), the
exhortations either on the first verse or at the beginning of the last verse (in
the last verse the call to 'come-all-ye' usually heralds some sort of moral or
warning to the listener) — all these recur with formal frequency and make the
student aware of the strict formula, albeit with minor shows of variation, of the
come-all-ye.

Gosport gives only a hint of grander things in the *genre*, for the English come-
all-ye never reached the heights of the Irish versions, splendid examples of

which are to be found, complete with tunes and contemporary wood cuts, in Colm O Lochlainn's two-volume *Irish Street Ballads*.

The lyric songs
It is always foolhardy to generalise and create national types, but within the loose framework of such generalisations there do indeed exist honest characteristics and true idiosyncratic features. Within the wide spectrum of folk song, it is probably safe to say that Scotland and the north-east of England produced the best narrative ballads, and that central and northern England, together with the western seaports, produced the most vigorous industrial songs and sea-shanties. That left another folk song type, the lyric song, to find its way around the country and to build its nest where it could.

The south of England, bereft of the bleak drama of the ballad-nurturing northlands and the tough breeding ground of the broadside ballad and industrial song, was a natural harbour for the lyric song, and, as it happens, most of the songs gathered in these shires is of the lyric type.

Lyric folk songs are not ballads: they do not tell stories, and they certainly do not tell heroic stories. Their function is to express feelings and their form and feature is elegiac. In Hampshire, as I have already said, the lyric folk song is rather like the county's gently-rolling downs. Not a great deal happens in the lyric songs of old Hampshire, which does not mean to say that there is not great beauty in the quiet poetry of her songs. Possibly their strongest quality is their power to evoke time and place and this they do to remarkable effect. Lyric songs are known up and down the country, and further afield; but in a county whose only mode of expression (and I'm laying aside the war songs of the Royal Navy at Portsmouth for the time being) is the lyric, Hampshire has produced relatively few native songs but has come to rely on the incursion from other counties of 'outsider' songs which Hampshire singers have adapted to local needs. There is little in the 'Hampshire' lyric, apart from some words, expressions and place-names, to distinguish it from the lyric from, say, Derbyshire or Somerset.

The Isle of Wight has given character to those lyric songs which have crossed the narrow strip of water which separates it from the rest of old Hampshire. Island songs, which are found commonly on the mainland, have taken on Island inflections and Island names; but by and large, *The Farmer's Boy* (hardly a real folk song, but a great favourite with real folk singers) is the same on the mainland as it is on the Island. And so it is with the songs of the mainland county and those of the rest of the country.

Sheepshearing, ploughing and cow-driving songs, fox-hunting songs, drinking and gambling songs, poaching songs, and, above all, courting songs (sometimes with a cunning allegory thrown in to delude the unwary) are the stuff of the Hampshire folk singer's songbag. In common with the rest of England, there is good and bad in the pile.

A common muse has guided the creation of most lyric songs and, in this context, there are close parallels with the lyric traditions of other countries. For it is in the lyric song that the soul of a people is most clearly shown, and we can see their hopes and fears, their dreams and sorrows and their expressions of love and hatred laid out before us. The language of the lyric song is more introvert, more subjective than that of some other folk song types, and yet it still manages to speak for a wider community than the single person. It is a language unknown to the commercial song-makers of Denmark Street and Shaftesbury Avenue.

Most peoples have developed and grown up in an atmosphere of ancient

18

Mummers — these are the Overton Mummers in 1944. They wear the elaborate disguises traditionally used to conceal the identities of the actors. Costumed used by other mummers frequently had decorative emblems sewn in, more to add colour to the garments than to disguise the wearers.

religious and superstitious beliefs and we have not yet thrown off the remnants of this prehistoric culture, despite our courtship of twentieth-century materialism. We still observe annual festivals such as Christmas and Easter and Hallowe'en and we still practice ceremonies which, though heavily disguised now, have echoes of a distant past. Our love-affair with fire is a primitive response: not so long ago fires were lit on the hill-tops of the southern downs; Hampshire villages carried out the 'firing the anvil' ceremony every year; and when we set light to the brandy-covered Christmas pudding, we perform a ceremony carried down from Roman times. The lighted candle in the window at Christmas is a pagan remnant as, indeed, is the sacrificial mass of the Roman Catholic church.

Sacrifice, as an intercession to the gods for a successful harvest or for a relief from pestilence, has moved away from the offering of human life to the traditional offering of farm and stall produce at our yearly Harvest Festivals. On the Isle of Wight 'Harvest Whoams' were eagerly-anticipated gatherings to celebrate the turning of the year. Many of our favourite folk songs survive because they were part and parcel of that village tradition. For an excellent reconstruction of an Island harvest home, we cannot do better than look at W.H. Long's *Dialect of the Isle of Wight* (1886), written at a time when these festivals were still commonplace.

Lyric songs, rather than ballads, were also featured in the winter mumming plays. These were short morality plays carried around villages, pubs and 'big houses' by a troupe of village players. The plays have survived in many forms all over the country and Hampshire is particularly rich in this tradition. We tend nowadays to regard the annual visit of 'the mummers' as an amusing prelude to Christmas, but in bygone days there was little to be amused about so far as the mummers themselves were concerned. These villagers took part in the plays as a means of bolstering their meagre wages in preparation for the expenses of the coming season. A certain amount of shame was attached to having to seek money in this way and some mummers went to great lengths to conceal their identities behind elaborate disguises, thereby attracting the nickname 'guisers'.

The plays were brief and performed to a rigid pattern. A number of characters appeared, including Father Christmas, a hen-pecked husband, a doctor with a bottle of life-restoring elixir, a Turkish knight (or 'turkey snipe' in some versions) and St George of England. After St George slew the knight and the doctor restored the dead man, the company completed their performance by singing Christmas songs and a selection of old traditional songs, often associated with the play or with Christmas. A collection was taken and the players rushed off to the next venue. This is how it used to happen, and this is how it happens today, except that the collected money is now usually donated to some charity. It is a tradition which nearly but didn't quite die out, and we have the modern revival of interest in folk song to thank for its survival.

Modern 'folk songs'

Is it possible to write a new folk song? With a few reservations, I'm inclined to say 'Yes', it is. At least we can imitate the style, the language, the form and features, and we can imitate the performance. In fact, some people have done this to a remarkable degree of success and we include some of their efforts in this book.

We have already dealt with the definitions of folk song and need not dwell for much longer on this need — if there *is* a need — to define it more clearly. But one last point requires to be considered. Sharp and the other collectors and folk song philosophers believed that a song needed the test of time to determine whether it would become a folk song in due course. Well, I'm afraid that longevity is no criterion for a song's qualification to be called a folk song. Just as many old folk songs which have survived the rigours of time are not very good songs by any stretch of the imagination, so we can be sure that a great many fine songs have disappeared from our tradition. You only have to look at the Child ballads to see how many have slipped out of common usage; you only have to leaf through Sharp's own impressive collections to see what we have lost.

I agree that, like an old house an old song takes on different characteristics and mellows with age, becoming in the process something quite different from that which it was when its creator sent it on its way. But who is to say that the song in its original state, in the mouth of its very first singer, was not already a folk song in every sense of the word other than 'ancient'?

It is my belief that folk songs can be written today and, knowing all the pitfalls of such a statement, I feel strongly enough about such a stance as to wish to give you examples. These new writers have chosen themes which are in keeping with the concept of this book as a memorial to Hampshire's past, and so they have written songs which concern themselves with life in our county's bygone days, thoroughly researching their material before setting pen to paper.

By choosing such long-lost themes we can at least see the lichen already gathering on the walls.

20

Performing the songs
Before we get on with the songs themselves, we really must spend a few moments considering how best they might be performed. Folk song is a remarkably resilient art form, quite capable of standing up to all sorts of treatment. Over the years it has sprung from the lips of trained concert singers, singing to piano accompaniment, and it has known the benefits or otherwise of the modern electronic and laser device. One notable recording artist once said that a folk song in the mouth of a trained singer is not a folk song at all. The same artist (were he still alive) might also have said that a folk song dressed up as rock music is no longer a folk song. There are degrees of truth in both attitudes, but we mustn't be too precious about all this.

This book is for singing songs from and it is really up to the individual performer to decide how he or she wishes to sing these songs. I have quite deliberately chosen not to arrange them, but to present them in their most basic form in the manner in which I first heard them. Were I to sing these songs, the duration of notes, the inflections and intonations would almost certainly be quite diferent from any interpretation which you might put on them, and so it should be, for we are not clones. My own preference would be to sing the songs unaccompanied, for in most cases this is how I first heard them and few English traditional singers accompanied themselves on musical instruments while they sang. John England, for example, who gave Cecil Sharp his very first folk song, *The Seeds of Love* all those years ago, failed to recognise the song when Sharp played it back for him on the piano! This had less to do with Sharp's ability to produce a recognisable facsimile than the transposition of the song from one idiom to another.

But in this day of the guitar, and the amplified guitar at that, few of my readers may wish to sing unaccompanied. It is a special skill after all; but the modern performer may much prefer the sound of the accompanied, arranged song and therefore I have included guitar chords. It's up to him or her, wherever you are. Here are the songs. Just try to remember what they are and where they have come from and how long they have been with us. We don't need to be too poker-faced about them, but I think they are entitled to a little respect. Handle them with care and, who knows, you may well be the one who keeps them alive for another generation.

John Paddy Browne
Southampton, 1987.

The Battle of Trafalgar

If the great sea shanties of the mid-19th century belong to the commercial shipping lines operating out of Liverpool, Bristol and Glasgow, then the great patriotic songs of the sea come from the armed navy of Deptford, Plymouth and Portsmouth, and a handful of other Royal Naval ports. Portsmouth Harbour was — and still is — the great natural sea base of the British southern fleet; and Spithead, the anchorage between the mainland and the north-eastern shoulder of the Isle of Wight, was the launching pad for many an assault against 'the enemies of England'.

And if the sea shanties of the tea-trading clippers were distinguished by their sometimes coarse vigour, the songs of the British fleets were remarkable for their belligerence, for their stories of aggressive victories, and for a sense of pride and loyalty to comrades and commanders. In the folk songs of the British Army, we can find any number of parodies, satires and mutinous sentiments against leaders and companions: such songs are few and far between in the armed navy. There are exceptions, of course: *Andrew Rose*, with its horrific description of naval punishment, is well enough known to folk singers. But such songs *were* exceptional.

In 1805, Nelson took his fleet out from Portsmouth Harbour in another attempt to settle the 'French problem'. With Russia, Austria and Britain arraigned against Napoleon, the 'Conqueror' could hold out little hope of success against the British navy. Nelson defeated the French at the decisive battle of Trafalgar, but he paid for his victory with his own life. It was left to another commander, Wellington, to settle the French question once and for all at the battle at Waterloo in 1815.

England's exhultation at the defeat of Bonaparte at Trafalgar knew no bounds. It was marred only by Nelson's death on the *Victory*. A handsome column was subsequently erected in the centre of London as a token of the country's gratitude for the man who is now largely remembered by a less fervent population for his affair with Lady Hamilton, and for six words, facetiously taken out of context every time they're quoted: *The nation expects* and *Kiss me, Hardy*.

Nelson's ship, badly damaged in the battle but later carefully restored, is now a land-locked tourist attraction in Portsmouth and is open to admiring day-trippers. Even French visitors may safely walk aboard...

The Battle of Trafalgar

The last line of each verse is spoken.

Arise ye sons of Britain, in chorus join and sing,
Great and joyful news is come unto our royal King,
An engagement we have had at sea
With France and Spain, our enemies,
And we have gained the victory,
   Again, my brave boys.

On the Twenty-first of October at the rising of the sun,
We formed the line for action with each man at his gun;
Brave Nelson to his men did say
The Lord is with us this fine day—
Give them the broadside, fire away,
   My brave British boys.

Broadside after broadside our cannon balls did fly,
While our smallshot like hailstones upon their decks did lie,
Their masts and sails we shot away
Besides some thousands on that day
Were killed and wounded in the fray,
   On both sides, brave boys.

The Lord protect brave Nelson and mercy show his soul,
For nineteen ships the combined fleet lost in the whole;
The *Achilles* blew up amidst them all
Which made the French for mercy call,
But Nelson was slain by a musket ball,
   My brave British lads.

Hurrah, my valiant seamen, hurrah — we've gained the day,
We've lost our brave commander, upon the deck he lies;
With joy we've gained the victory
Before he died did plainly see
Old Spain and France for Mercy plea,
   My own British boys.

Now may this glorious victory bring on a speedy peace,
That all trade in England may flourish and increase,
That our ships from port to port go free
And as before with all agree,
And no more face an enemy,
   My brave loyal lads.

The Battle of Trafalgar

Beware Chalk Pit

The obelisk on top of Farley Mount can be seen for miles around; and when you have trundled up the long hill from Hursley village you are rewarded by a spectacular view across some of Hampshire's most verdant countryside, with not a town in sight and only the red bricks of Hampshire farm buildings far below your feet.

This is chalk country, and from time to time the traveller will pass by the odd disused chalk quarry, now overgrown with weeds and wild flowers, and inhabited by rabbits and huge black crows who have picked out tiny nest caves high up in the cliff faces.

It was while riding his horse one day in 1733 that Sir Paulet StJohn jumped into one of these bramble-covered chalk pits. What should have been a fatal accident left neither horse or rider impaired in any way, and Sir Paulet had the novel idea of renaming his horse *Beware Chalk Pit*.

The newly-named horse went on to win the Hunter's Plate at Winchester Races in Worthy Down, evidently none the worse for its experiences. A plaque on the inside of the monument (the second to have been erected in memory of Beware Chalk Pit) tells the whole story.

Graham Penny's song is in true Henry Newbolt style; he sings it on a Forest Tracks record, accompanying himself with a cantering rhythm on guitar.

Beware Chalk Pit

There's a tale I'll tell to you,
It's remarkable but true,
Of Sir Paulet St John and his noble steed;
An event which you shall see
Back in 1733.
Of which Hampshire gentlemen should all take heed.

Chorus
Beware Chalk Pit, beware Chalk Pit,
As you go galloping over the downs
Beware Chalk Pit. (Repeat all three lines)

As Sir Paulet rode to hounds
'Cross the rolling Hampshire Downs,
He was riding hard as he was wont to do,
When he jumped a bramble hedge
And went headlong o'er the edge
Of a chalk pit that was hidden from his view.

Chorus

Now the chalk pit's sides were steep,
It was twenty-five feet deep,
How they came upon it I cannot account,
But the strangest thing of all
—They both survived the fall
Without injury to rider or to mount.

Chorus

Now Sir Paulet knew, of course,
That the fault was not his horse,
And for riding blindly he should take the blame;
By all rights he should be dead,
Of his horse he proudly said
He shall henceforth be remembered by this name·

Chorus
Beware Chalk Pit, Beware Chalk Pit,
The finest horse in Hampshire,
Beware Chalk Pit.

Now when Chalk he passed away,
Well his master then straightway
Did on Farley Mount a monument erect,
And if you should pass that way
You can still observe today
This enduring final mark of his respect.

Chorus
Beware Chalk Pit, Beware Chalk Pit,
As you go galloping over the downs
Beware Chalk Pit.
Beware Chalk Pit, Beware Chalk Pit,
The finest horse in Hampshire,
Beware Chalk Pit.

Beware Chalk Pit

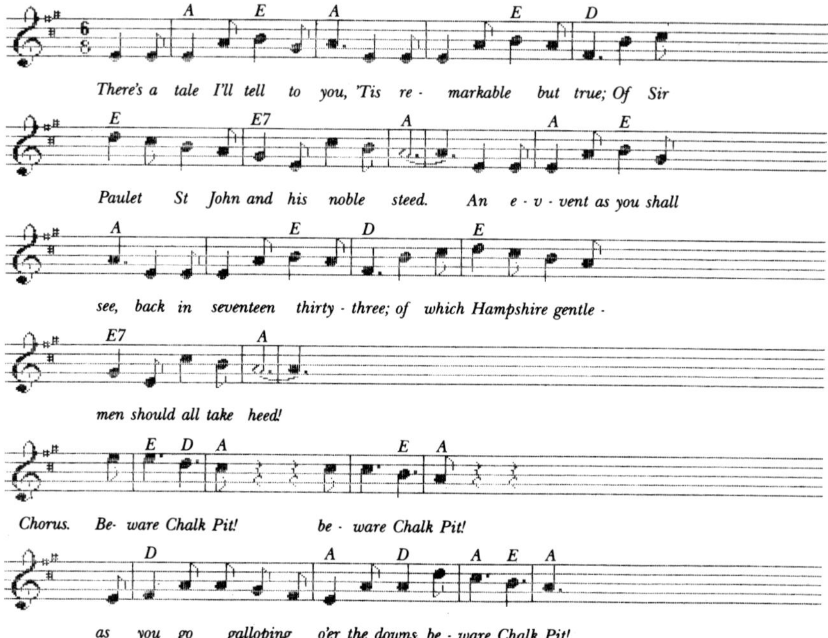

The Bonny Bunch of Roses

As a professional cartographer, I have always been fascinated at how the history of England is reflected in the map coverage of certain parts of the country at certain times. After the collapse of the second Jacobite Rebellion of Charles Stuart (Bonny Prince Charlie) at Culloden, there was a rash of maps of the 'troublesome' areas of Scotland. The maps of pre-Rebellion Scotland had proven to be of little use to an army on the march (or in retreat for that matter) and so a new programme of map-making was set in motion.

Map-making in Scotland was quickly abandoned, however, when a new threat to England raised its head in the form of Napoleon who seemed certain to invade the country through its southern counties. Suddenly there was a plethora of surveyors at work in Kent, Essex, Hampshire and Dorset, producing maps in preparation for the defence of the kingdom. The first Ordnance Survey map, published on the first day of the 19th century was, therefore, a military map of Kent. The other counties quickly followed.

The 'bonny bunch of roses' was an emblematic representation of England, Scotland, Wales and Ireland, though we can only wonder at what the ballad-makers of the day were talking about when they said 'their unity was never broke', for 'unity' between these countries has always been a sorely argued point.

Napoleon's defeat at Moscow curtailed his plans for the invasion of England, and we can only guess at the sense of relief which must have been felt — especially in these southern shires — as the news of his downfall spread throughout the land. There is a surprising element of admiration and even pity for "The Great Conqueror" in nearly all the so-called Napoleonic ballads — remarkable when we consider the strength of preparations to repel him should he have attempted his assault.

The ballad given here is widespread throughout these islands with variations in tune and text. In this story the 'young Napoleon' is the Duke of Reichstadt, who died at Schönbrunn in 1832: he is reflecting on 'The Conqueror's' downfall.

The Bonny Bunch of Roses

By the margin of the ocean one morning in the month of June,
The sweet and pretty songsters their charming notes sang
    in full tune,
I there espied a female who seemed to be in grief and woe,
Conversing with young Bonaparte about the bonny bunch of roses-o.

Then up stepped young Napoleon and took his mother by the hand,
Said, Mother dear, have patience until I'm able to take command:
I'll raise a powerful army and through tremendous dangers go,
And in spite of all the universe I will conquer
    the bonny bunch of roses-o.

Now son don't speak so venturesome, in England are
    the hearts of oak,
There's England, Ireland and Scotland whose unity was never broke.
And son, think of your father, in St Helena his body lies low,
And you may soon follow after him, so beware
    the bonny bunch of roses-o.

He took three hundred thousand men, with kings likewise
    to bear his train,
He was so well provided for that he could sweep the world for gain.
But when he came to Moscow he was overcome by the driven snow,
And Moscow was a-blazing, so he lost the bonny bunch of roses-o.

Now mother, fare thee well, adieu, for I am on my dying bed,
I might have conquered all the world but now
    it pains my youthful head.
But while my bones may wither and willow trees about me grow,
The deeds of bold young Bonaparte will sting
    the bonny bunch of roses-o.

The Bonny Bunch of Roses

The *Bounty*

On the morning of April 28, 1789, a group of men entered the captain's cabin on the armed vessel, *Bounty*, and declared that they were taking control of the ship. It was the start of one of the most famous and notorious episodes in British naval history.

What was to become known as The Mutiny on the *Bounty* had been brewing for some time. Leaving Portsmouth Harbour two days before Christmas in 1787, the *Bounty* had made a difficult passage to Tahiti under the command of Lieut (not Captain) William Bligh. Her mission: to gather a large quantity of seedling breadfruit plants and transport them to the British colonies in the West Indies where they were to be planted and grown as a cheap food for the slaves there.

Following a long and, by all accounts, idyllic sojourn on Tahiti, the *Bounty* set sail, loaded with the young plants, the mission all but successfully completed.

But the lassitude and amorous excesses enjoyed by the crew while on Tahiti had spoilt the men for the renewed hardships of life at sea. Added to this, the friction which sprang up between Bligh and his Master's Mate, Fletcher Christian, brought Christian reluctantly to the position of rebel leader. Christian had been appointed to his post at Bligh's recommendation; Bligh, in fact, thought Christian a young man of promise with a distinguished naval career ahead of him. We can imagine Bligh's disappointment at the sight of Christian's behaviour at Tahiti, and his dismay at finding himself awakened on that fateful morning by his neophyte holding a sword to his throat and uttering the threat *One word and you are dead, sir!*

Forever damned by a wildly fictionalised account by novelists Charles Nordhoff and James Norman Hall, and by an indelibly slanderous portrayal by Charles Laughton, Bligh was a more humane man and a far better sailor than Christian, and a less villainous figure than we perhaps might like to think of him. Deprived of his ship, Bligh was cast adrift on the open sea, in the *Bounty's* completely inadequate cutter, laden down to danger point by as many loyal supporters as Christian could cram in. Bligh made a heroic 4,000 mile voyage, bringing all his men except one to safety at Timor after forty-one days. Christian took the *Bounty* on an erratic course around the south Pacific, searching for a safe haven, and finally came upon Pitcairn's Island — quite by chance, for Pitcairn had been incorrectly plotted by all previous chart-makers. The mutineers burnt the *Bounty* on the island's rocky shore, and then proceeded to kill each other off (one of the first to die was Christian) until, rediscovered by a passing American sealer nearly twenty years later, only one man of the original twenty-two mutineers had survived.

The ballad adopts the traditional but historically inaccurate view of Bligh as tyrant and Christian as martyr to Bligh's villany. This suggests that the song is not so old as its style suggests: following Bligh's return to England the *Bounty* saga was even further sensationalised in a series of theatrical plays in which Bligh was very much the hero of the affair. Our ballad is sometimes sung to the tune used for *Death and the Lady*, a sobering and cautionary tale of the frailty of human vanity which has parallels in Hamlet's soliloquy to Yorick's skull.

Bligh of the Bounty. *Despite the image of him as tyrant foisted on us by fiction-writers and Hollywood films, he was more humane than even Nelson and Cook, and a far better sailor than Fletcher Christian.*

The Bounty

From Portsmouth Harbour we did set sail,
The glass was high and foretold a gale,
For fair Tahiti we sailed away
To drop our anchor in Matavai Bay.

The *Bounty* was a noble craft,
Copper-fastened both fore and aft,
Her masts were lofty and full of sail,
Her rigging bound as we bore away.

Well, soon the Needles we left from view,
And to old England we bade adieu,
Old England that we loved so well,
To cross the seas in this floating hell.

When we came close by to Staten Land,
For four long weeks we made our stand;
'Brave boys, brave boys,' old Bligh did cry,
'Pull on full square and we'll pass her by.'

But that's one thing that was not to be,
We could not break that raging sea;
'Pull hard about,' our captain swore,
'We'll spend our strength on this no more.'

Well, when Australia hove into view,
For Adventure Bay our course we drew,
The *Bounty* for a while did stand,
For drink and rest by Van Deiman's Land.

'Haul up, me boys,' old Bligh did cry,
'There's far to go and the sea is high.
Haul up me boys, with a right good will
And at Tahiti you may rest your fill.'

And at Tahiti we did alight,
And what we say was a wond'rous sight:
Those native girls came down in flocks
With their skin of gold and their coal-black locks.

Three cheers went up from each sailor bold,
When all these beauties we did behold;
With kind affection they bid us land,
And every comfort was at our command.

For five long months we lingered there,
And to stay forever was each man's prayer;
But Captain Bligh to our deep dismay,
Cried 'Up, me bully boys, we must away.'

'Twas in the year of eighty-nine,
To leave Tahiti he was inclined,
Our captain's word we must now obey,
And them that failed — well, they rued the day.

Well, on those seas for New Holland bound
The men on board heard a dreadful sound:
'On deck, on deck,' Bligh did command,
'And them that's slow, they will feel my hand.'

And when we all had assembled there,
Young Fletcher Christian was in deep despair;
The captain's anger he bore full sore
For the robbing of the captain's store.

That night when all was peace and still,
Young Christian swore he would have his will,
And when old Bligh rose up from his sleep
There were swords and pistols at his bed-feet.

'Rise up, rise up, my captain bold,
This day your blood is to run cold,
Be up on deck with every man,
For now this ship is at my command.'

No mercy did our captain crave,
And no mercy did we to him give,
With one small craft on that ocean wide
We cast him overboard and out of sight.

Now all you seamen that do pass by,
Remember Captain William Bligh;
Remember Fletcher Christian too,
And the blood that flowed on that sea of blue.

The Bounty

From Portsmouth Harbour we did set sail, The
glass was high and foretold a gale For fair Tahiti we
sailed away To drop our anchor in Matavai Bay.

PITCAIRN ISLANDS
6d
H.M. ARMED VESSEL "BOUNTY"

Buttercup Joe

The rural worker has been the butt of as many jokes and caricatures as, say the mean Scot, the fighting Irish, the singing Welshman, or whatever. Lampooned on countless music-hall stages, the country labourer has been portrayed as a simple bumpkin, albeit with a streak of cunning. Dozens of Variety Show artists have made decent livings out of this image of the farm labourer as village fool: Sir Bernard Miles and Billy Burden come swiftly to mind; and dozens of monologues and songs have adopted the theme.

Few of these songs are folk songs in the true meaning of the term, but many have become part of the country singer's stock and are now, paradoxically, folk songs of a sort.

Buttercup Joe is the archetypal country bumpkin song. It is known all over the country and is popular enough to have any number of locations substituted for 'Fareham'. I have heard 'Wareham', 'Sarum' and 'Thakem' versions. Town dwellers, when they sing the song, affect their own ideas of the country dialect, the end result being about as true to the authentic farm worker as the words are. Nobody, however, not even countrymen, seems to take offence.

Music halls provided a range of entertainment which included jugglers, comedians and — in this case — acrobats. They were the forerunners of the variety shows which went out of fashion after the Second World War. Music hall and variety shows often featured 'rustic' singers and entertainers delivering such songs as Buttercup Joe *and* The Farmer's Boy. *These songs may not have been* bona fide *folk songs, but they quickly found favour with real folk singers who added them to their repertoires.*

Buttercup Joe

Now I be a rustic sort of chap,
My mother lives o'er Fareham,
And my mother she's got lots more like I,
For she knows how to rare 'em.
Some they calls I Bacon Fat,
And others Turnip Head,
But I prove to you I be no mug
Because I'm country bred.

Chorus
Now I can guide a plough, milk a cow,
And I can reap and mow,
Fresh as the daisies in the fields
And they calls I Buttercup Joe.

Now I suppose that you all knows
About my little Mary:
Her works as busy as a bumbly bee
In Farmer Jones's dairy.
Now don't her make them dumplings good,
By Christ, I means to try 'em,
And I'll ask her if she'd like to wed
A lusty chap like I am.

Chorus

Reaping...

...and mowing

Buttercup Joe

Down Hampshire Way

'The song will not make its effect unless it is sung in moderately slow time, and with a certain dignity...'

So it said in the *Hampshire Advertiser and Southampton Times* of July 2, 1927, when the song was published over a whole page. The words are by Hugh Scott and the music, by Dr Heathcote Statham, doesn't tell us how to overcome the change of rhyme and metre in the second verse!

Newspapers in the south of England are not very good at publishing songs of their own area. Certainly folk songs have never found favour with southern newspaper editors, although there has always been a place for the amateur versifier. Papers and magazines in other parts of the British Isles have shown a better understanding of the value of folk song. One regional newspaper, *The Tyrone Constitutional*, published a weekly folk song, with tonic solfa settings, for so many years that the collection finally became one of the most respected anthologies of folk songs in these islands, and is known as *The Sam Henry Collection* after the man who organised the feature for 17 years.

Songs like *Down Hampshire Way* were written for various types of celebratory function and sometimes became very popular within certain circles. *The Anacreontic Society*, for example, had its own ritual drinking song; the Oxford and Cambridge Boating Clubs had theirs and, of course, at the other end of the scale, every rugby club has its own songs. Such songs may not be folk songs *per se*, but their popularity and longevity, as well as their singability, lend them some of the qualities of folk song. The excuse for including a song such as *Down Hampshire Way* is tenuous, but its attraction is irrepressible.

Down Hampshire Way

I'm Hampshire bred and Hampshire born,
And proud of it am I,
No softer, purer air I know
Beneath God's boundless sky.
If sylvan glades of forest shades
Or moorland be your call,
Or country, town or sea or ships,
Old Hampshire has them all.
   Go east, go west, old Hampshire's best
   And all therein is fine,
   If Hampshire highways and byways are my ways,
   They always will be mine!

The stranger never need feel strange
When he's within our bounds,
We'll welcome him till soon he feels
On old familiar grounds.
Deny it if you can —
For Hampshire folk are kind and true,
For work or play or worth or love —
Just try a Hampshire man!
   Go east, go west, etc.

Of olden cities nobly placed
Upon the scroll of fame,
Southampton, Portsmouth, Winchester
All bear a wond'rous name.
And Bournemouth as our Beauty Queen
The world doth recognise,
So young and old and rich and poor
Fair Hampshire's name will prize.
   Go east, go west, etc.

Down Hampshire Way

Drink old England Dry

Ever since the first public houses opened their doors, I dare say, their clientele found the need to express themselves in song and rousing chorus, especially as the evening mellowed and grew more convivial. As the bar's spirits go down, so the customers' spirits rise and by evening's end everyone thinks that he can sing like Caruso.

England, in common with most nations, has celebrated the pub — or more correctly — the discovery of alcoholic refreshment in song, and some of the country's best songs are drinking songs. The effects of the various temperance groups over the years has had little impact on the drinking classes, but the Womens' Temperance League did inspire a rather good selection of neo-folk songs of its own, with strong moral tones and hair-raising choruses. The celebrated Victorian illustrator, George Cruickshank, made a decent living out of drawing fearsome pictures for songsheets and books in which the evils of drink were driven home with sledgehammer subtlety.

Drink old England Dry is a typical lusty song of its type, best sung with a strong-voiced chorus singing in close harmony. In this way it can sound like the tap-room on Saturday night and, at the same time, like the front parlour of a temperance meeting.

And if you are confused by the words which speak in the first verse of the French threatening to invade England, and in the second verse of Lord Roberts, you have reason to be: this is one of those examples in which a folk song from one period takes on bits of another song from a different period. Thus we have verse one referring to the Napoleonic war, and verse two referring to the Crimean war! More recent versions even mention Churchill.

Drinking old England dry... this seems to have been the worst threat posed to Englishmen since time immemorial! The song has been around for a long time, embracing different periods in an odd juxtaposition. During the Second World War, versions were collected which featured Churchill.

Drink old England Dry

Come, me brave boys, as I've told you before,
And drink, me brave boys, and we'll boldly call for more;
For the French they would invade us and they say that they will try,
They say that they will come and drink old England dry.

Chorus:
Aye dry, aye dry me boys, aye dry,
They say that they will come and drink old England dry.

Well up spoke Lord Roberts, that man of high renown,
And he swears he'll be true to old England and the crown;
For the cannons they will rattle and the bullets they will fly
Before they'll ever come and drink old England dry.

Chorus

Well, suppose that we should meet with the Germans on the way,
Ten thousand to one we'll show them good old British play,
With our swords and our bayonets we'll fight them till we die,
We'll die before we let them drink old England dry.

Chorus

Drink old England Dry

The Dummer Sheener's Gang

Dummer, just off the M3 south of Basingstoke, came out from sleepy obscurity in 1986 when one of its young ladies, a Miss Sarah Ferguson, married Prince Andrew, second son of Queen Elizabeth II, and became the Duchess of York in a spectacular wedding ceremony which captured the attention of millions of television viewers across the world.

Dummer basked in the reflected glory of the occasion and, for a time, left behind the village way of life which gave rise to such songs as this. The song is parochial, concerned only with the village and those characters of the village sufficiently interesting to be enshrined in a song. As such, the song is a pure 'come-all-ye', and, although it names only local inhabitants and local events, it is interesting for the insight into local *mores* which it evokes. It is, in short, part of a potted history of a small part of the county, and thus of England.

It was given to me by Bob Copper who learned it from Frank Bond of North Waltham, a local man who had travelled widely with fairground people and who, according to Bob, had acquired a certain air of sophistication,. Frank, for example, knew that he carried in his head a respectable repertoire of songs of interest to people such as folk song collectors and his reasoning was that if collectors were likely to make any money out of his songs, then he should have his share. I don't suppose Frank realised just how little money there is to be made from folk song collecting!

'Sheen', incidentally, is a contraction of the word 'machine' and a 'sheener' is a man who works on a threshing machine. The song describes the various chores carried out on this useful piece of farming equipment.

Bob Copper, erstwhile landlord of the HH Inn at Cheriton and folk song collector for the BBC. He and his family have been responsible for preserving many of the songs of old Hampshire. His reminiscences of song-collecting days in the county are vividly recorded in his book Songs and Southern Breezes.

The Dummer Sheener's Gang

I'll sing you a song of a sheener's gang,
I've got 'em all taped up to a man,
There's long and short and thin and fat,
But every man knows just what he's at.

Chorus
Sing fal-the-ro lai-rum
Fal-the-ri laddie-i-day.

Six o'clock comes we now begin,
We usually stops 'twixt nine and ten,
To oil her up and see all things right,
And she'll knock out a couple of ricks by night.

Chorus

Jimmy Bailey he runs the concern,
He's got plenty of wood and coal to burn,
He pulls the lever and makes her grunt,
And the wheels we'll keep on going for a month.

Chorus

There's Brewer Allen the sheaves to put,
A lively gait he must keep up.
Old Chin keeps snipping the bonds all day,
And Butler he hucks the caven away.

Chorus

Ernie Annetts is 'baggin the hoiles',
He is always handy when Jimmy calls,
He don't belong to the sheening crew,
But comes to oblige for a day or two.

Chorus

There's big, old Long'un and Plummer Hide,
On the corn rick working side by side,
They takes it easy, 'tis play for they,
Supplying old Brewer with sheaves all day.

Chorus

There's Sammy Elmer and old Tom too,
A-hauling the corn and got plenty to do,
They've got a sack-lifter of great renown,
And you squeezes a handle to steady her down.

Chorus

There's Wiggy and Mush building the rick,
To see 'em at work, well, it's a freak,
They builds 'em round or square or flat,
And tops 'em up the shape of your hat.

Chorus

Now sheeners thrived in the days of yore,
When work was hard and money was poor,
And if you were grafting for Hillary's delight,
'Twas from two in the morning till ten at night.

The Dummer Sheener's Gang

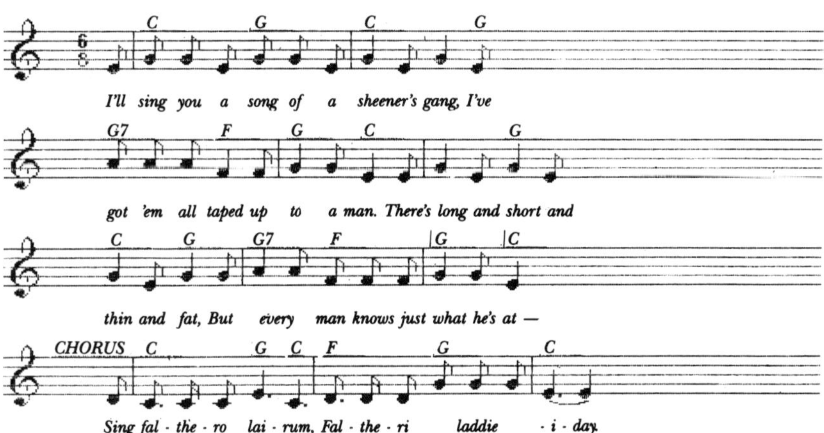

The Execution of Frederick Baker

The usual (sic) quiet town of Alton, Hampshire, was on Saturday evening drawn into a state of intense excitement owing to a report being current that a horrid murder had been committed on a child named Fanny Adams, between seven and eight years of age. The rumour, on enquiry, unhappily turned out to be too true...

So reported *The Police Gazette* on the events of 24 August 1867, which introduced a new expression into the English language and into common usage — Sweet Fanny Adams.

The circumstances of the death of little Fanny Adams (actually, she was eight years and four months old) were particularly harrowing, and her murderer, when they caught him, could expect little mercy.

Frederick Baker had apparently lured Fanny into a corner of Horace's Field — later to be a housing estate — and after what he himself described as a 'fine and hot' murder, dismembered her body and scattered it far and wide. He was, however, arrested later that same day and brought to trial before Mr Justice Mellor at the Winter Assizes held in Winchester Castle. He was found guilty of Fanny's murder and sentenced to be hanged at the city's prison.

'This morning,' one of the many broadsides of the day reported, 'the wretched criminal Frederick Baker suffered the extreme penalty of the law at Winchester Prison for the atrocious murder of Fanny Adams. It is satisfactory to state that since his condemnation, the conduct of the unhappy man underwent a total change for the better, and his demeanour was changed into one of deep dejection.'

The broadside describes how Baker, a former solicitor's clerk, was attended by the chaplain and the sheriffs; how the procession was formed and slowly took its way to the scene of execution; and then *'the cap and rope was (sic) adjusted, the bolt drawn, and the prisoner was launched into eternity.'*

As an aside, this record of the slow procession to the gallows differs from the description of the hangman's business told by Albert Pierrepoint in his autobiography. Pierrepoint, the most famous of all England's official executioners, tells us that at the first stroke of eight o'clock he could enter the condemned man's cell, pinion the victim's arms, walk him out of the cell and up the gallows steps, place a hooded mask and the rope over his head and have him dead before the clock had struck the eighth chime.

No-one now remembers the name of Frederick Baker but the name of Fanny Adams has become part of our folklore. At best it is used to describe something which is hopeless; at worst it is a profanity. Even the Royal Navy uses it to describe a certain type of canned mutton.

Whichever way her name is remembered nowadays, it is a sad memorial to an unfortunate and innocent little girl.

One last reflection on the reliability of broadsides: the sheet titled *Execution of Frederick Baker for the Wilful Murder of Fanny Adams* gets the date of the murder wrong by three days. Fanny Adams is buried in Alton cemetery.

The Execution of Frederick Baker

You tender mothers pray give attention
To these few lines I will now relate,
From a dreary cell to you I mention
How a wicked murderer has now met his fate.
This villain's name it is Frederick Baker,
His trial is over and his time has come,
On the gallows high he will meet his maker
To answer for that cruel deed he's done.

On that Saturday little Fanny Adams
Near the hop-garden with her sister played,
With hearts so light, they were filled with gladness,
When that monster, Baker, towards them strayed;
In that heart of stone not a spark of pity
As he those halfpence to the children gave,
But now in gaol in Winchester city
He soon will die and fill a murderer's grave.

He told those children to go and leave him
With little Fanny at the garden gate.
He said, Come with me, and she believing,
In his arms he lifted her as now I state.
O do not take me, my mother wants me,
I must go home again, please sir, she cried,
But on this earth she never saw them,
For in that hop-garden there, the poor girl died.

When the deed was done and that little darling
Her soul to God her maker it had flown,
She could not return to her mother's bidding,
He mutilated her, it is well known.
Her heart-broken parents in anguish weeping,
For vengeance on her murderer cried,
Her mother wrings her hands in sorrow,
O would for you, dear Fanny, I had died.

The jury soon found this monster guilty,
The judge on him this awful sentence passed,
Saying Prepare yourself, for the cruel murder
You have committed, your die is cast.
And from your cell you will mount the scaffold,
And many thousands will you behold,
You will die the death of a cruel murderer,
And may the Lord have mercy on your guilty soul.

What visions now must haunt his pillow
As in his cell he does lie the while?
She calls to him, O you wicked murderer,
'tis I your victim calls, that little child!
The hangman comes; hark, the bell is tolling,
Your time has come, you cannot be saved.
He mounts the scaffold and the drop is falling,
And Frederick Baker fills a murderer's grave.

*The murder of sweet Fanny Adams. The child had been lured into a field by Frederick Baker
and slain in (to use Baker's own words) 'a fine hot murder'. Our picture is from* The
Illustrated Police News *a journal which treated the most gruesome and bizarre items of news
with awesome detail.*

The Execution of Frederick Baker

George Collins

George Collins has been found in several parts of the country but not so frequently as it has turned up in Hampshire. The song's mysterious elements — never fully explained by folk song experts — create an eerie surrealism which parallels that of another mysterious song, again usually found in Hampshire, called *The Streams of Lovely Nancy*.

The plot of *George Collins* is almost exactly the same as that of the Child ballad *Clerk Colvill*. In both, a young man meets a strange woman by a riverside; she is of some supernatural quality for, as a result of the meeting, the man dies. A number of other women also die at the same time, all of them with a knowledge of Collins. We are never told how or why all this should happen, but there is a temptation to recall *The Churchyard Bride* (see my notes on *The Gosport Tragedy*).

George B. Gardiner found at least four versions of *George Collins* in Hampshire in 1906. Our text is based upon two fragments supplied to Gardiner by Henry and Philip Gaylor of Minstead, near Lyndhurst. The tunes used for the song may be as widespread as the words, with variants turning up in *Lord Lovell*, *The Outlandish Knight*, *Lord Thomas and Fair Elinor* and *Giles Collins*, the latter being a close musical relative of *George Collins*.

George Collins

George Collins rode out one May morning
When may was all in bloom.
There he espied a fair pretty maid
A-washing a marble stone.

She whooped, she halloed, she highered her voice,
And she held up her lily-white hand;
'Come hither to me, George Collins,' said she,
'For thy life shall not last thee long.'

George Collins rode home to his father's own gate,
And loudly he did ring,
Come rise my dear mother and make my bed,
Rise, father, and let me in.

For if I chance to die tonight,
As I suppose I shall,
Bury me under that marble stone
That joins fair Elinor's hall.'

Fair Elinor sat in her room so fine
Working her silken skein,
When she saw the fairest corpse a-coming
That ever the sun shone on.

She said unto her servant maid,
'Whose corpse is this so fine?'
'This is George Collins' corpse a-coming,
That was once a true lover of thine.'

Come, put him down, my six pretty maids,
And open his coffin so fine,
That I might kiss his lily-white lips,
For a thousand times he kissed mine.

And go upstairs and fetch me the sheet
That's woven with silver twine,
And hang it over George Collin's head,
Tomorrow it will hang over mine.

The news was carried to London town
And wrote all on London gate,
That six pretty maidens died all on that night,
And all for George Collins's sake.

George Collins

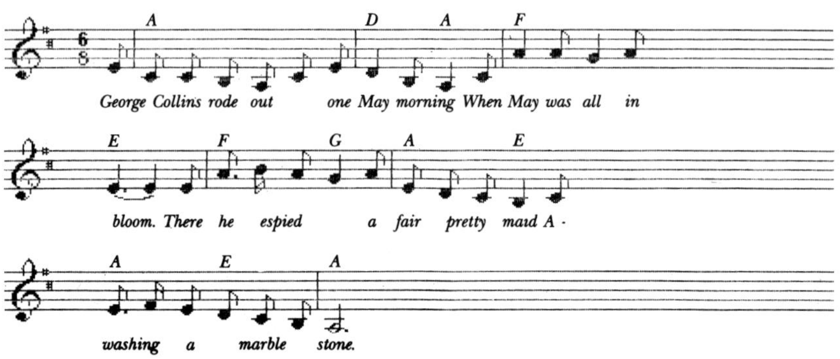

Gosport

This is a 'come-all-ye' — one of those peculiar songs which concern themselves with parochial and domestic themes but which dress unremarkable occasions in the garb of grander events. This folk song *genre* is the most commonly found song species of all, appealing to the ear rather than to the poetic senses.

Having said that, the come-all-ye can rise to higher things and at its best it can take on the mantle of real poetry. Literary merit is, however, not the purpose of the come-all-ye whose function is to get a simple story across simply. The *genre* originated in Ireland and came to England with Irish migrants fleeing the famine of the mid-nineteenth century.

English forms of the come-all-ye have lost much of the exaggerated florid style of the Irish originals: in *Gosport*, for example, you will find only traces of the insistent internal rhymes which characterise the older forms, and much of the elaborate allusion to classical themes which dominate the Irish come-all-ye has been watered down in our ballad. Nevertheless, we can still find the odd hint of all this in the mention of Naples, Venice and Rome.

The tune for *Gosport* was written by Richard Leveridge, the words by Henry Man, and the song (which first appeared in a broadsheet of 1765) was sung by Leveridge at the theatre in Lincoln's Inn Field, London. Other versions of the song, with different tunes, exist.

Nowadays, the term 'Come-all-ye' is often used in folk clubs to signify an evening to which anyone can come along and sing a song or two.

The Royal Marine Barracks at Gosport at the turn of this century.

Gosport

I sing not of Naples, of Venice, or Rome,
Of the pillar of Trojan or Peter's fine Dome;
Neither praise I old Brentford, that place of renown,
But will sing of a seaport, and Gosport's the town.

And the inns are so noble, so neat and so clean,
If you talk of a mop they scarce know what you mean;
All infection however, they keep from their doors,
With tobacco juice sprinkled to sweeten the floors.

The want of fine buildings and grand collonades
Is made up by fine women and good-humoured jades,
Though the lasses of pleasure, take black, fair or brown,
Scarce amount to ten thousand in all Gosport town.

Then the tars who get drunk such civility show
That by daylight you sometimes in safety may go;
And though after dark you are sometimes knocked down,
There are plasters in plenty in Gosport's good town.

So polite and so social the people are here,
They'll converse with their friends once or twice in a year,
By friends I mean those of an equal degree,
For why should great folks with inferiors be free?

At balls and assemblies such wisdom is shown,
All distinctions and stations are easily known,
For each officer's state, as good breeding contrives,
Is copied with care and kept up by their wives.

The police is so perfect such order is kept,
Law and gospel, long time have so silently slept,
That e'en Justice herself does not care to appear,
Having long since been drowned in a butt of strong beer.

But adieu to his worship, to Gosport adieu,
Though a theme more delightful no muse could pursue,
For the coach is prepared to set off from the Crown,
So I'll finish the praises of Gosport's sweet town.

(After each verse, the Chorus goes:
Derry down, down, down derry down).

Gosport

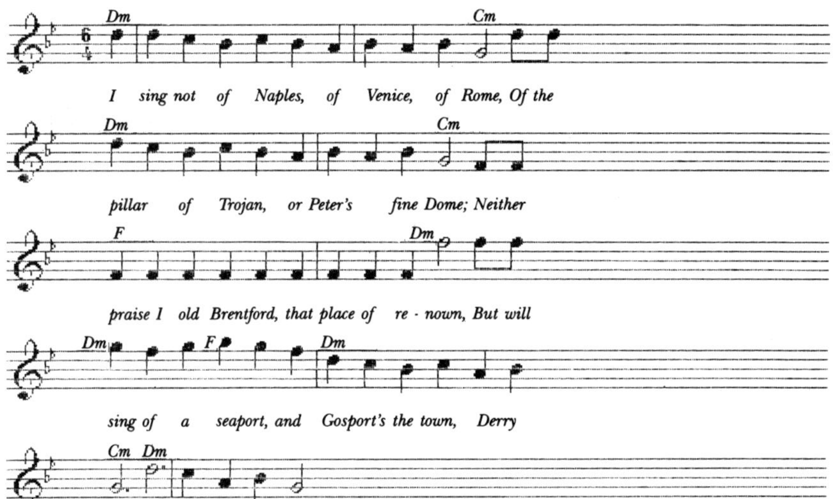

Down, Down, down derry down.

Henry V and the King of France

When, in the middle of Henry V, Shakespeare moves his scene to the eve of departure for France and the Battle of Agincourt, the action on that eve takes place in Southampton. We are in the very heart of the old town and many of the relics of those days are still to be seen: the Bargate, where two conspirators against Henry were executed for treason; the Red Lion public house where it is alleged (but unconfirmed) that the conspirators were tried; Blue Anchor Lane and Westgate Street down which the king's troops marched to embarcation; and the twin gates of Blue Anchor and Westgate which opened out to the sea.

Local legend has it that the Black Death entered England through the Westgate in 1348, but the same claim is also made for Melcombe Regis in Weymouth, Dorset.

In those days the sea licked the town walls of Southampton. It was long before Pirelli's and municipal swimming baths and ring roads pushed the Solent almost out of sight. It is difficult to imagine, as you walk along Western Esplanade today, that you tread on land that was once a seafaring race's stepping-off place for the four corners of the globe, since time immemorial down through the Pilgrim Fathers and their little *Mayflower,* to the great armadas of D-Day in the Second World War.

The history book versions of the events leading up to Agincourt are — or should be — well enough known to every English schoolboy. What is less well-known is the folklore version. Apparently, a sort of mutual 'protection racket' operated between France and England, each king taking it in turn to provide the other with some suitable gift of land or gold or ships or whatever, in return for peace.

When Charles VI sent the young Henry a set of tennis balls as France's offering for 1415, Henry was so unamused that he assembled his armies and set out for France and a confrontation with Charles at Agincourt. The tennis balls were coated in concrete — or whatever substitute they had then — and used as ammunition in the battle. It was all too much for Charles: Henry beat him hands down, got the 'ten tons of gold' which he should have been sent in the first place, and married Katherine of Valois to boot.

Shakespeare makes great play of the tennis balls sequence, and it is rumoured that until quite recently a number of these concrete missiles had been housed at the Tudor House Museum, the old timbered building which stands at the top end of Blue Anchor Lane.

(See also my notes for *The Woolston Ferry*).

Henry V and the King of France

As our king was lying all in his bed
A certain thought came to his head,
That he would send to the king of France
And cause his tribute to be paid.
   Right fol de rol, fol di right fol re.

Arise my page, my trusty page,
My trusty page arise to me,
And you will go to the king of France
And bring the tribute due to me.

What news my page, my trusty page,
From English king what news to me?
O I have come from the English king
To bring the tribute due from thee.

Your king is young and of tender years,
And has not come to my degree,
So I will send him some tennis balls
That with them he might play, might he.

Arise my page, my trust page,
My trusty page arise for me,
And we will send him such tennis balls
That in fair France they never did see.

Recruit me Cheshire and Lancashire
And Derby men that are so free,
But no married man and no widow's son,
For no widow's curse shall fall on me.

They recruited Cheshire and Lancashire
And Derby men that are so free,
And when their numbers were counted o'er
There were forty thousand men and three.

They fought the French and they fought the king
Until they gained the victory,
They fought the kind until he cried
Have mercy on my men and me!

O I will send your tribute home,
Ten tons of gold is due to thee,
And the fairest lily that grows in France
To the Rose of England give I free.

Henry V and the King of France

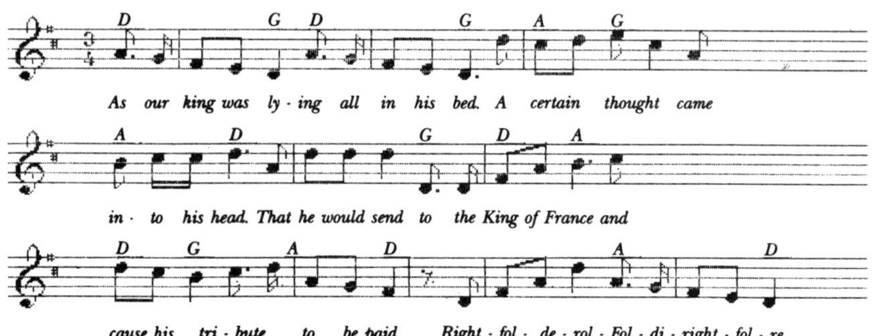

I'm a Bold and Rambling Soldier

The south of England has a lot to thank Napoleon for. Had it not been for him, it's unlikely that the British Army would have made such a home of these counties. True, there had always, it seems, been trouble and strife with the Continentals, but it took old Boney to put the wind up the government. It was his threat of invasion (see also *The Bonny Bunch of Roses*) which brought the army in droves to Hampshire and Wiltshire and Sussex, to set up a line of defences to keep 'The Corsican' out. The little matter of Moscow prevented the English defences ever having to be put to the test, but an anti-Napoleon line was still effectively in place when, years later, Hitler cast a greedy eye at the white cliffs of Dover and at what lay beyond.

To this day, vast tracts of southern sward is out of bounds to the public, or access is severely curtailed, as the army munches its way over chalklands and rabbit warrens and deserted villages, their massive tanks and artillery practice creating a new brown landscape from England's green and pleasant land. To give credit where it is due, we should concede that if the army didn't own all this lovely open space (which they *do* let us walk across between firing times), the whole of southern England would by now almost certainly have fallen under the spreading rash of the property developer's red brick and white concrete.

Aldershot is the home of a very large section of the British Army, and the army, like the navy and the air force, has always produced a fair copiousness of songs, many of which are quite emphatically folk songs. As is the case with sailors' songs, those of the other services fall into two main categories: work songs and leisure songs. The leisure songs can be further divided into sentimental, recreational or entertainment songs, tall tales or bawdy ballads. And where a lot of men get together socially, their songs tend towards the latter — *vide*, rugby socials — and so it has been, it seems, since the dawn of time.

The last World War, like the so-called 'Great War' of 1914-18, produced a vast new catalogue of songs, some of which were mere adaptations of earlier repertoires. Field Marshal Montgomery's racy advice to this troops on the code of conduct for 'horizontal refreshment' seemed to give official sanction to the behaviour of many of the fictional deeds or wishful thinking of the more chauvinistic soldier songs, of which this one is fairly typical.

A version of this song was collected by Gardiner at Micheldever, Hants, in 1906, but the words differ slightly from those given here.

I'm a Bold and Rambling Soldier

I'm a soldier blithe and gay and I'm rambling for promotion,
I've fought the French and Spaniards now for miles across the ocean;
I've travelled England and Ireland through,
I've travelled bonny Scotland too,
And there's many a maid I've caused to rue
The bold and rambling soldier.

When I was young and in my prime, for years I went recruiting,
In England, Ireland and Scotland too, just to avoid the shooting,
With a lady fine and a charming life
And in every town a different wife,
Why, rarely was there any strife
With the bold and rambling soldier.

At Aldershot I courted Jane and her sister and her mother,
And all the time that I was there, they were jealous of each other;
When our orders came I had to start,
I left poor Jane with a breaking heart,
And at Aldershot she had to part
With her bold and rambling soldier.

Well now the war is over and I'm not ashamed to mention
The king has given me my book and with it comes a pension;
There's many a maid will cast the blame
Though few of them will know my name,
For that, me boys, was all a game,
I'm a bold and rambling soldier.

I'm a Bold and Rambling Soldier

Jack the Painter

The story of Jack the Painter, incendiary extraordinary, who set fire to Portsmouth's dockyards, is a remarkable tale and the inspiration for this song by Hampshire singer Brian Hooper.

James Aitkin, alias Hinde, earned his nickname during his apprenticeship to an Edinburgh painter. Aitkin was born in Edinburgh in 1752 and enlisted at Gravesend at the time of England's war with America. He made quite a career of dockyard blazes, making use of his time between his many desertions from the forces, and his equally numerous re-enlistments, to survey naval ports and to make his pyrogenic attacks on them.

When he set fire to the rope-house at Portsmouth he caused a spectacular blaze — but it was to be his last. Captured and tried at Winchester, he was sentenced to be hanged from the yard of the *Arethusa*, within sight of the remains of his last bonfire. Legend has it that the rope used to hang him was a fragment left over the rope-house fire.

After the execution, his body was taken to Blockhouse Point in the harbour and hung in chains for several years. At some time later his dried bones were stolen by a group of sailors, placed in a sack and taken to Gosport where an unwitting publican, accepting the mysterious sack as surety for an evening's drinks, doubtless received an unpleasant shock when he opened it up.

Some say that the ghost of Jack the Painter haunts Portsmouth Harbour and that the rattle of his chains may be heard on a windy night.

Brian Hooper's song was pre-dated by an earlier anonymous ballad which began:

> Whose corpse by pond'rous irons wrung
> High up on Blockhouse Beach was hung
> And long to every tempest swung?
> Why, truly Jack the Painter.
> Whose bones some years since taken down
> Were brought in curious way to town
> And left in pledge for half-a-crown?
> Why, truly Jack the Painter.

Brian's song takes its style and flavour from the narrative form of the old ballad sheets and would have looked well on one of those grotesque broadsides.

Jack the Painter

At the mouth of Portsmouth Harbour, where the old chain ferry plied,
Some say a spirit hangs in chains, where submarines now glide,
Though his bones have gone, the Devil knows where,
Jack the Painter lingers there,
Now Painter Jack's just bones in a sack, but the Dockyard's working yet.

Though Jack he was a painter, as a brand he made his name,
He met his fate in Portsmouth, where he set the 'yard aflame,
But the firemen bold and the seamen brave,
Doused the flames, the fleet to save,
Now Painter Jack's just bones in a sack, but the Dockyard's working yet.

At Winchester the trial was held and sentence it was passed,
Jack hanged at the gate of the Dockyard, from the *Arethusa's* mast;
Though the rope store stood a blackened wreck,
There was rope enough for the painter's neck,
Now Painter Jack's just bones in a sack, but the Dockyard's working yet.

In chains he hung at Blockhouse Point, and stayed for many a year,
'til taken to an alehouse as a pledge to pay for beer,
So if you've no money, just a body in a sack,
You can try for a pint on Painter Jack,
Now Painter Jack's just bones in a sack, but the Dockyard's working yet.

Repeat first verse (last line twice).

Jack the Painter

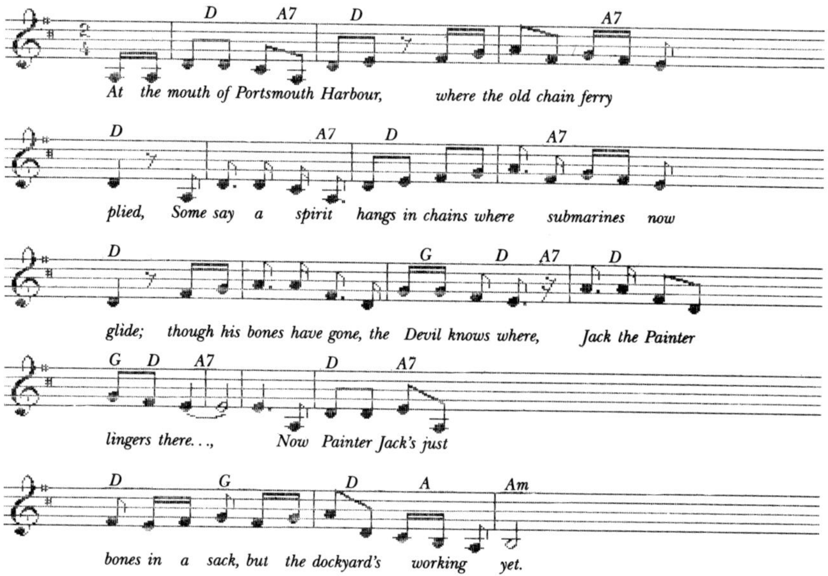

The Knife-and-Scissors Man

Graham Penny is one of the most prolific song-makers in Hampshire, creating songs which are an evocation of the past and the people who inhabited that past. His songs are more than that, however; for although they may mention Hampshire place names, (Beaulieu, the New Forest, Farley Mount, the old School of Navigation at Hamble, the River Avon at Christchurch, and so on) the songs can conjure up pictures from all of our days past. Those of us old enough to remember a knife-and-scissors man trundling his little cart through our streets will identify with Graham's wan figure walking the back streets of Southampton.

Such a quality is the essence of the true folk song: it is at once an objective thing and yet it speaks for every one of us. Bugle Street in Southampton, apart from the modern buildings, is very much the same Bugle Street of many generations ago: the *Duke of Wellington* is one of the town's oldest public houses, and it still serves a decent pint. At the bottom end of the street is the sea; behind us is the Bargate, the storied gateway to the town. In between is St Michael's Church, the town's oldest ecclesiastical building and once a beacon for seafarers who can still spot its lofty spire from miles away; the Tudor House, once the home of a lord who gave his name, *My Lord's Lane*, to the street which is now known as Blue Anchor Lane; and Blue Anchor Lane itself, down which Henry V marched part of his army on their way to Agincourt.

Graham Penny's song may concern itself with lesser moments in history than all this, but his history is even more tangible and immediate.

The Knife-and-Scissors Man

In Southampton's former days
When grandma was a maid
And people used to ride the horse-drawn trams,
Every other Friday came
A man to ply his trade,
It was Pedlar Jack, the knife-and-scissors man.

Chorus
Bring your knives and scissors out,
I'll sharpen them for you,
They'll last until I come around again.
Bring your knives and scissors out,
I'll make them good as new,
Broken knives, broken scissors I can mend.

From street to street he made his way,
His living he'd to earn,
His funny old machine upon his back,
He'd set it down and pedal it
To make the grindstone turn,
That's why the people called him Pedlar Jack.

Chorus

He covered all the streets between
The Bargate and the Pier,
He'd doff his hat to every passer-by,
And at the *Duke of Wellington*
He'd take a glass of beer,
Then Bugle Street would echo to his cry.

Chorus

Customers he never lacked,
Both rich and poor alike
Always knew they'd get their money's worth,
If his machine had only been
A penny-farthing bike
He might have cycled half-way round the earth.

Chorus

How the children loved to see
The grindstone meet the blade,
It always seemed to take them by surprise,
They'd stand around in wonderment,
Watch the sparks cascade
Mirroring the twinkle in his eyes.

Chorus

The Knife-and-Scissors Man

Mars for Evermore

This belligerent song mentions the *Agamemnon* in its refrain. The *Agamemnon* was, with the *Illustrious* and the *Swiftsure*, the most famous and largest ship to be built at the now-defunct yards at Bucklers Hard, close by Beaulieu. The proximity of the New Forest ensured a plentiful supply of English oak and other timbers — the primary building material in pre-steam days.

The *Master Builders* hotel-cum-public house in Bucklers Hard displays a roll of honour of ships built and launched from the hamlet's yards into the Beaulieu River.

The *Agamemnon, Illustrious* and *Swiftsure* were all engaged at Trafalgar and Nelson was at one time captain of the *Agamemnon*. In fact, it was during his term of command of this vessel that he lost his right eye at the siege of Calvi.

(See also my notes on *The Battle of Trafalgar* and *Nelson's Death*.)

Mars for Evermore

Well now, brave boys, we're off to the main,
    Roar, Agamemnon, roar,
To load our ships with the dollars of Spain,
    Mars for evermore!

They tell us thirty ships of the line
    Roar, Agamemnon, roar,
From France and Spain on the sea do shine,
    Mars for evermore!

Those ships of France and Spain my shine,
    Roar, Agamemnon, roar,
But they'll not forget the year '05,
    Mars for evermore!

The guns did rattle and the shot did hail,
    Roar, Agamemnon, roar,
And every ship fought fire and flame,
    Mars for evermore!

The streams of blood from their scuppers did flow,
    Roar, Agamemnon, roar,
The blue sea ran with purple gore,
    Mars for evermore!

We'll burn their boats and flatten their mountains,
    Roar, Agamemnon, roar,
We'll make their blood to flow like fountains,
    Mars for evermore!

Well from our guns blew the British thunder,
    Roar, Agamemnon, roar,
And that's how we keep our enemies under,
    Mars for evermore!

Mars for Evermore

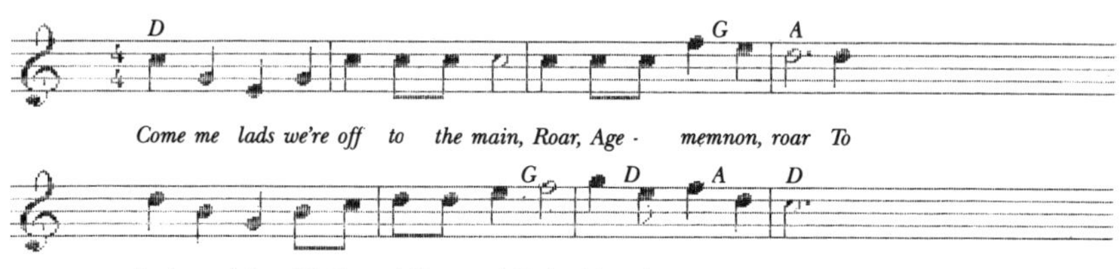

The Monmouth Rebel

Ringwood has had unpleasant associations with the Civil War in England, for it was here that the Duke of Monmouth, en route to the coast and safety after the rebellion of 1685, was captured. A short distance north of Ringwood is Ellingham where Dame Alicia Lisle is buried in St Mary's churchyard. At the age of 80, she was condemned to death by Judge Jeffreys for harbouring fleeing Monmouth supporters after the battle of Sedgemoor. Taken from her home at Moyles Court, just east of Ellingham, she was beheaded at Winchester.

Moyles Court is now a school.

Brian Hooper wrote the words and tune for this fine song which attempts to 'get inside' the mind of the fictional rebel who escaped the bloody azzises of Judge Jeffreys.

A fresco showing the arrest of Dame Alicia (or Alice) hangs in the lobby of the House of Commons.

The Monmouth Rebel

I wasn't but a growing boy when first I came to arms,
Behind the Duke of Monmouth in the march across the West,
The troops they came to stop us, and we used our country charms,
But the troops they sent to Sedgemoor were the best, the very best,
The troops they came to stop us, and we used our country charms,
But the troops they sent to Sedgemoor were the best, the very best,

They chased us through the ditches and they brought us to the court,
But to hear so many men would take three seasons of the year,
So confessions they were traded for a trip across the sea,
Better transport there than face the gallows here, the gallows here,
So confessions they were traded... etc

When the pardon came from London, to New York I made my way,
And found myself a freighter ship, to bring me home in style;
The journey was so pleasant that I scarcely was prepared
To hear what did befall my Lady Lisle, Lady Lisle,
The journey was so pleasant... etc

She came before a circuit judge, and Jeffreys was his name,
With no-one to defend her, and a jury bought for gold;
For sheltering a minister who fought the same as I,
She's lying now so silent and so cold, and so cold,
For sheltering a minister... etc

She was threescore years and twenty when she came to the Assize,
And I was just a rebel boy who never faced a trial;
I'm thankful for my pardon, but it brings me pain as well,
For it came a bit too late for Lady Lisle, Lady Lisle,
I'm thankful for my pardon... etc

Repeat first verse

The Monmouth Rebel

Nelson's Death

Horatio Nelson was born in 1758 at Burnham Thorpe, Norfolk, the son of a poor rector. Both father and son were plagued by constant illness, so much so that at the age of only twelve, young Horatio was sent out to work for his living. An uncle, Captain Maurice Suckling of the Royal Navy, scoffed at the idea of the weakling lad being sent to sea but subsequently relented, saying 'Let him come, and the first time we go into action a cannon-ball may knock off his head and provide for him at once.'

When young Horatio finally arrived, unaccompanied, at Chatham, he wandered around, cold, wet and hungry, unable to find his uncle's ship. No-one had been told to expect him. . .

From such an unpromising beginning came the figure who was to become one of England's most celebrated national heroes. A long list of successful campaigns against different enemies led to Trafalgar and to Nelson's moment of glory. At the age of 47, he was shot dead on board his flagship *Victory* within sight of his triumph over the French and Spanish fleet in 1805.

It is difficult for us now to imagine the sensation the *Victory* and the death of Nelson caused in the country, although we saw glimpses of this reaction in the aftermath of the Falklands campaign. For a hundred years after Trafalgar, an eager public bought relics and trinkets celebrating Nelson, the *Victory*, and the Battle of Trafalgar. But the dawn of even more gruelling conflicts, which led ultimately to two savage world wars, tended to shove the idolatory of 'national heroes' into the background, and wars began to be seen for what they are — not glorious and heroic, though glorious and heroic deeds and people may emerge from them — but bloody, cruel and uncivilised.

Nelson is buried in St Paul's Cathedral, London, within a cannon-shot of the handsome column erected in his memory at Trafalgar Square.

The song (there were many about Trafalgar, the *Victory*, Nelson, and Nelson's final moments) mentions another of the hero's victories — at the battle of the Nile in 1798. Collingwood was Nelson's second-in-command on the *Victory*, and it was he who despatched the note to the Admiralty which announced Nelson's death.

(See also my notes on *The Battle of Trafalgar* and *Mars for Evermore*.)

Nelson's Death

Poor Britain's long expected good news from the fleet,
Commanded by Lord Nelson the French for to meet;
Till at length the news came over, through the country was spread,
That the French were defeated but Nelson was dead.

Not only brave Nelson, but thousands were dead
They had gone with the French to their watery bed;
And to save our poor country's honour and wealth
They fought with the French and they fought them unto death.

Our plans for the victory are brilliant and good,
A monument for Nelson and for brave Collingwood;
Let them be of fine marble and honour their fame,
And say of Lord Nelson, 'He died in England's name'.

Our soldiers and sailors their brave deeds have done,
While fighting the foe many battles have won;
If the Nile could but speak or Trafalgar declare,
They would say there was nothing with Nelson could compare.

Nelson's Death

DEATH OF NELSON
in the Cockpit of the Victory.

The Outlandish Knight

This song is wide-spread throughout Britain, but what distinguishes this version (which I collected partially in Lymington) is the fussiness of the language. The text sung for me had all the marks of the 'improver'. Now, improvers are people who, faced with either the tunes or text of folk songs —or both — can't believe that what they see and hear is correct, so they take it upon themselves to 'improve' the tune or the lyrics. Many folk song collectors in the past were guilty of wholesale alterations to words and tunes although we should admit that, in the case of the words, the moral climate of the period in which they lived largely enforced these changes. The songs which suffered most in this respect were those dealing with the delicate subject of encounters between the sexes. Sometimes the alterations were so dramatic as to completely obscure the meaning of the original song; in a number of cases only the tunes were preserved and set to quite different sets of words.

The Outlandish Knight is one of the ballads first brought to our attention by the pioneering work of Professor Francis J. Child whose 5-volume collection *The English and Scottish Popular Ballads* was first published in the United States in 1898. Child listed all known variants of the ballads still in existence in Britain at the time, and most folk song students today refer to these ballads by the sequential numbers as they appear in the collection. *The Outlandish Knight* was known to Child although in Child's work it is sometimes called *Lady Isabel and the Elf Knight* and (Child 4) *The Gowans Sae Gay, May Colvin* and *The Water o' Wearie's Well*. This all gives you some idea of how complex a path folk ballad research can be.

Folk *ballads* differ from folk *songs* in this respect: the ballads tend to be narrative in form, telling stories and recording events of some importance, whereas the songs — or lyrics — tend to be expressions of feelings. Hence *The Outlandish Knight* tells us about an encounter between a naive lady and her opportunist lover.

The ballad has undergone more than textual change with the passage of time. Our version is typical of the best-known forms of the ballad, but more complete versions continue the story with a parrot witnessing the murder of the knight and threatening to reveal the lady's crime if certain favours are not forthcoming. Perhaps the fantasy element of this part of the ballad was too much for the ballad-singers to put across convincingly and for this reason they decided to drop it. At any rate, most people today only sing the truncated version.

The Outlandish Knight

An outlandish knight came from the north land,
Came a-courting of me,
He promised to take me back to the north land
And married there to be.

Go fetch me a case of your father's gold
And some of your mother's fee,
And the two best horses in the stable
Where there stand thirty and three.

And bring me a case of your father's gold
And some of your mother's fee,
That we might have fortune all in good store
When we get to the north country.

He mounted on the milk-white steed,
She on the dappled grey,
And all that night they rode and they rode
Till at last they came to the sea.

Dismount, dismount, my fair lady!
Deliver that gold to me,
For six pretty ladies I have drowned here
And the seventh you are to be.

And also take off that lovely dress,
Deliver it also to me,
For I say that it is too fine and gay
To rot with you in the sea.

If I have to take off my lovely dress
Then turn your back on me,
For I will not allow that a ruffian as you
A naked woman should see.

Then he turned his back on the lady so fair,
And bitterly she did weep,
Then she caught him around the waist so small
And she flung him into the deep.

Lay hold of my hand, my fair lady!
Lay hold of my hand, cried he,
That I might be saved and you be my bride
When we get to the north country.

Lie there, lie there, thou false-hearted man!
Lie there instead of me;
For six pretty ladies you have drowned here,
But the seventh one has drowned thee.

The Outlandish Knight

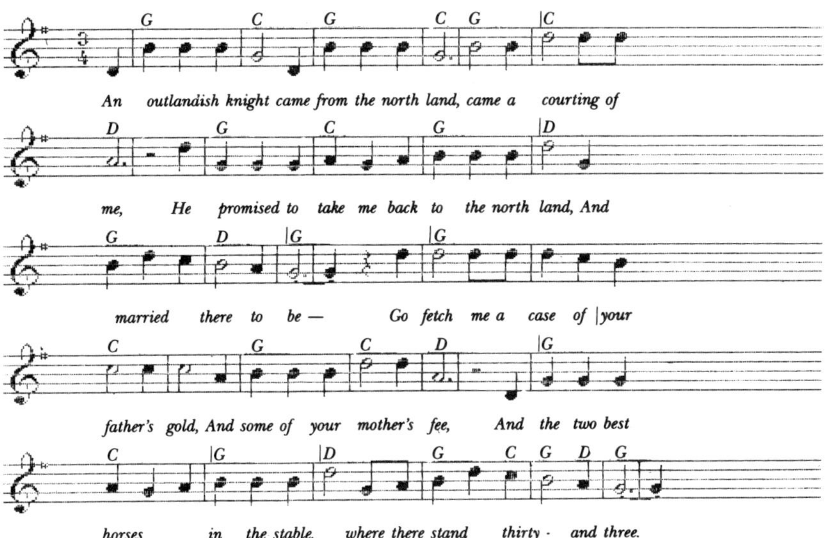

The Owslebury Lads

The hamlet of Owslebury, a few miles south-east of Winchester, was the scene of one of the last labourers' revolts against mechanisation of agricultural work. In 1830 — not 1813 as the ballads would have us believe — a group of farm labourers took it upon themselves to wreck a quantity of new machinery, threshing machines mainly, which they felt posed a threat to their livelihood. Following the affray at Owslebury, 245 men were arrested and brought to trial at Winchester. Many were sentenced to transportation or to terms of imprisonment with hard larbour; two of the convicted were hanged.

E.J. Hobshawm and G. Rudé, in their book *Captain Swing* (1969), fill in some of the details surrounding the events of the time. Our song is the only one concerning the labourers' revolt in the south of England which has come to light. Where were our local songwriters then?

Approaching the hamlet of Owslebury, scene of the destruction of farm machinery, as the Industrial Revolution reached agrarian Hampshire.

The Owslebury Lads

The thirteenth of November, eighteen hundred and thirty,
The Owslebury lads they did prepare all for the machinery,
And when they did get there, my eye! how they let fly,
The machinery flew to pieces in the twinkling of an eye.

Chorus
The mob, such a mob, you have never seen before,
And if you live for a hundred years you never will no more.

O then to Winchester we were sent, our trial for to take,
And if we do have nothing said, our counsel we shall keep;
But when the judges did begin, I'm sorry for to say
So many there was transported for life and some was cast to die.

Chorus

Some times our parents they comes in all for to see us all,
Some times they bring tobaccy or a loaf that is so small;
Then we goes into the kitchen and sits all around about,
There is so many of us in there that we all be soon smoked out.

Chorus

At six o'clock in the morning our turnkey he comes in
With a bunch of keys all in his hand tied up all in a string,
And we can't get any further than back across the yard,
With a pound and a half of bread a day,
    now don't you think that hard?

Chorus

At six o'clock in the evening the turnkey he comes round,
The locks and bolts do rattle like the sounding of a drum,
And we are all locked up again all in our cells so high,
And there we stay till morning, whether we live or die.

Chorus

And now for to conclude and finish with my song,
I trust you gentlemen round me will think that I'm not wrong,
And all the poor in Hampshire for rising of their wages
I hope that none of our enemies will ever want for places.

The Owslebury Lads

Rolling Home

Here's a song that most old salts seem to know in one form or another. It doesn't have the language of the folk song, but despite its musical kinship to the gospel song and its literary flavour of the drawing room, it has always been a favourite with sailors. Not surprising; for men who have wrestled with the sea, despite all their toughness and occasional profanity, have a deep-rooted faith, possibly born out of their respect for this most enigmatic and dangerous of elements. A life-long proximity to death helps to purify the soul.

Captain W.B. Whall in his famous collection *Sea Songs and Shanties*, first published in 1927 when the songs were still fresh in his mind, gives us a version of *Rolling Home*, and he says that he has another version dated 1876. John Masefield, a former poet laureate and author of that memorable schoolboy sea-song:

Dirty British coaster with a salt-caked smoke stack,
Butting through the Channel in the mad March days...

— has published another version. So the song has been around for a while.

Stan Hugill, probably the last of the old professional shantymen, in his magnificent *Shanties From the Seven Seas*, gives three long versions of the song, including one in German with the traditional English chorus adapted to read 'Rolling home to dear old Hamburg...'

The song is not a shanty, but is a 'forebitter' or 'fo'c'sle song', used by sailors when off duty.

Our version comes mostly from the singing of the late Bob Roberts, who used to describe himself as 'a sea adventurer'. One of the last commercial Thames bargees, he once told me that he only visited places he could sail his boat into. When he retired from active sea life, he steered into the Isle of Wight and made berth there. The author of several books, he once sailed the Atlantic single-handed in a 26-foot cutter. Just before his death he recorded a number of his favourite sea songs and *Rolling Home*, which he said he often heard on ships coming up the Channel towards their Hampshire ports, is among them.

The tune resembles the American Civil War song *The Vacant Chair* and the Irish 'rebel' song *Kevin Barry*.

Rolling Home

Call all hands to mend the capstan,
See the cable is all clear,
For tonight we sail for England
And for England sure we'll steer.

Chorus
Rolling home, rolling home,
Rolling home across the sea,
Rolling home for dear old England,
Rolling home, dear land, to thee.

Let us heave with a will, boys,
And the cable we will trip,
And across that southern ocean
We will steer our gallant ship.

Chorus

Man the bars with a will, boys,
Let all hands that will press on,
And as we heave around the capstan,
Let us sing our homeward song.

Chorus

To Australia's lovely daughters
Let us bid a fond adieu,
We will not forget the hours
That we spent along with you.

Chorus

A thousand miles now lie behind us,
A thousand miles no more to roam,
Soon we'll see our dear old country
And the place where we were born.

Chorus

Round Cape Horn one winter's morning,
All among the ice and snow,
You could hear them shell-backs singing
Steer her home, boys, let her go!

Chorus

Cheer up, Jack, bright smiles await you
From the fairest of the fair,
From the wives and gals who's waiting
Standing there upon the pier.

Chorus

Rolling Home

The Shepherd's Song

Gardiner found three versions of this song in Hampshire — at Winchester, Alresford and Micheldever, and Frank Purslow liked it enough to include it in his excellent little book *Marrow Bones*. He tells us that the song has been found in many parts of the south and this is not surprising considering that its subject is likely to have found favour with the sheep farmers who work the chalk downs of our region.

The song captures the essence of the south and manages to combine the Hampshire countryman's care for his flock (after all, it *is* his livelihood) and his love for the good beer of the Strong Country. The famous brewery may no longer exist but the memory lingers on.

The Shepherd's Song

We shepherds are the bravest boys that treads old England's ground,
If we go into an alehouse we value not one crown;
We'll call for liquor merrily and pay before we go
While our sheep lie asleep, O where the stormy winds do blow.

Come all you valiant shepherds that have got valiant hearts,
That goes out in the morning and never feels the smart,
We'll never be faint-hearted, we'll fear no frost or snow,
We will work in the fields, O where the stormy winds do blow.

As I looked out all on the hill, it made my heart to bleed,
To see my sheep hang out their tongues and they begin to bleat;
And I plucked up my courage bold and up the hill did go,
To drive them to the fold, O where the stormy winds do blow.

And now I have a-folded them and turned back again,
I'll join some jovial company and there be entertained;
A-drinking of strong liquor, boys, which is our hearts' delight,
While our sheep lies asleep, O full safely all this night.

The Shepherd's Song

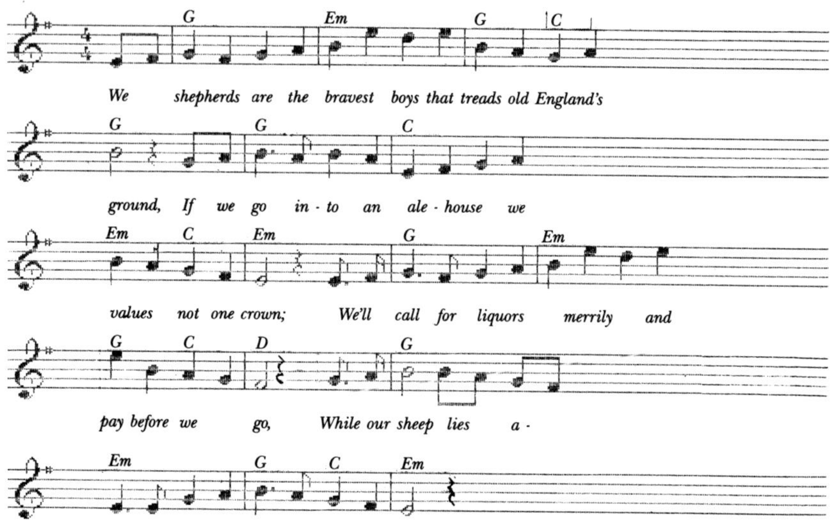

The Ship in Distress

Cannibalism at sea has never been encouraged, glad to say, but neither is it unknown. *The Ship in Distress* was a well-known 'fo'c'sle' song (that is, a song sung by sailors in off-duty hours, usually below decks), and was frequently found by researchers combing the repertoires of merchant navy singers. Such versions often had melancholy endings; the uniformed sailor favoured the Royal Navy rescue at the end of some other versions.

William Makepeace Thackeray wrote his *Little Boy Bill-ee* in the 19th century, possibly after having heard *The Ship in Distress* . He anticipated the fate of the unfortunate 17-year old Richard Parker of Peartree Green, Southampton, who had booked as cabin boy on an unseaworthy yacht in 1884 and ended up being knifed to death and eaten by his three shipmates when the boat, en route for Sydney, Australia, foundered in a storm. The four men had taken to the yacht's dinghy but had quickly run out of food.

After the sixteenth day adrift the hapless quartet had already discussed the possibility of three of them living off the flesh of the fourth, and they proposed drawing lots to see who would die first. Parker inadvertently solved the problem by drinking sea-water and becoming violently ill. Taking advantage of this, the 32-year old captain of the yacht, a Thomas Dudley from Colchester, killed Parker with a penknife, and the three lived off the corpse for a further five days until picked up by a German ship.

Parker's remains were buried at sea; the others were brought to trial at Falmouth but all escaped with lenient sentences. A memorial stone was in time erected to Parker over his mother's grave in Peartree churchyard, within a rivet's throw of the shipbuilding yards at Woolston, just over the steep hill in front of the church.

Woolston, a place of interest in its own right, was also the home of the famed *Spitfire* fighter plane of the Second World War. Until recently, the town was linked to Southampton proper by an inelegant but functional cable-drawn floating bridge. This clanking, rumbling machine was so admired by the Lancashire artist, L.S. Lowry, that he painted its portrait (it's in Southampton's art gallery), and it also inspired a song with this memorable if unprophetic chorus:

The Woolston Ferry doesn't travel very fast,

It was never built for comfort, it was built to last.

Thackeray's poem, despite attempts by the author to standardise it, has undergone several changes and has been set to various folk and folk-like tunes, one of which became popular in Hampshire folk clubs in the 1960s and is due for a dusting-off. If Thackeray's *Little Boy Bill-ee* was a parody on a tragedy, the variants foisted upon him have been further parodies:

There were three men of Portsmouth City
Who stole a ship and went to sea;
There was Guzzling Jack and Gorging Jimmy
And also Little Boy Bill-ee.

They sailed across the broad Atlantic
And all they'd left was one split pea;
Said Gorging Jack to Guzzling Jimmie
'I am extremely hun-gar-ee.'

Said Gorging Jack 'I'm going to eat you,
We've nothing left, we must eat we.'
Said Guzzling Jimmie 'I'm old and toughish,
So let's eat little boy Bill-ee.'

Said Gorging Jack 'We're going kill and eat you,
Undo the top button of your chemie.'
When Billy heard this information
He drew his pocket handkerch-ee.

'O let me say my catechism
That my dear mother taught to me.'
He climbed up to the main top gallant,
And there he fell on bended knee.

And when he reached the fifth Commandment
He cried 'Yo-ho, it's land I see!
I see Jerusalem and Madagascar
And North and South Americ-ee!

I see the British fleet at anchor,
And Admiral Napier, KCB!'
And when they climbed aboard the flagship
They hanged fat Jack and flogged Jim-ee.

The floating bridge — or ferry — has now been replaced by a lofty concrete bridge which may not be as romantic as the old moving bridge or offer the same sense of apprehension (the old ferry occasionally broke its moorings and drifted downstream), but it affords more spectacular views of the surrounding countryside and reduces the time taken to cross the river.
(See my notes on *The Woolston Ferry*).

The Ship in Distress

You sailors bold who sail the ocean
See dangers landsmen never know;
While some gain glory and promotion
No words can tell what we undergo.
While on through storms and the heat of battle
There's no back door to run away,
While thundering guns and cannons rattle
Mark well what happened the other day.

A merchant ship by Captain Divers
A long time had been out at sea,
The weather being dark and stormy
We were driven to anxiety.
There was nothing left for these souls to cherish,
Through lack of food most feeble grown,
When my poor messmates were almost perished
With nothing left but skin and bone.

Their cats and dogs had all been eaten
Their hunger for to ease, we hear,
And in the midst of all their sorrow
Both men and captain took equal share.
But now a dread has overcome us,
A dismal dread most certainly,
Poor fellows, how they stood in torture
Casting lots for who should die.

The lot it fell on one poor fellow
Whose family was very great
And which did the more increase his sorrow
For to repent was far too late.
I well may die, but brother messmates,
Climb to the masthead straightaway
And see if you a sail discover
While I my last few prayers pray.

Well there's a sail I spy to westwards,
It's bearing down to our relief.
When these few blessed words came to us
They quickly banished fear and grief.
God bless that ship and her brave captain,
Who gave us life to tell the tale,
For by his great and friendly actions
To Lisbon we did safely sail.

The Ship in Distress

The Southampton Tragedy

'What has brought me here?' asked Abraham Baker of the chaplain of Winchester Gaol. The melancholy Baker was executed on January 8, 1856 for the murder of Naomi Kingswell in the large house at Moira Place, Southampton, where she had been employed as a domestic maid. In a letter found after his execution, Baker answered his own question: 'Pride, not reading my bible, Sabbath breaking and all manner of wickedness.'

Baker, a native of the Isle of Wight, had fallen hopelessly in love with Naomi while both lived on the Island, and they travelled together to Southampton where he became footman to the Reverend William Poynder of Moira Place, an elegant Victorian terrace now long-since demolished but which stood at the junction of Above Bar Street and New Road, opposite the present-day cinema.

We will probably never know what brought about the confrontation between Baker and the girl 'on whom he had promised marriage'; staff at her residence suspected nothing and had no idea that relations between the lovers had reached such a dangerous state. Without warning, and in full sight of the cook, Baker shot the 22-year-old Naomi through the head. Baker offered no resistance when placed under arrest by a passing policeman.

The circumstances of the murder caused a sensation in the town; and as Baker's former devout and good-natured character was revealed in his trial, a great wave of sympathy arose in his favour. Even the judge, Baron Parke, who sentenced the unhappy Baker to death, remarked: 'You allowed jealousy to take possession of your mind and to overpower those feelings of reason and religion which you seem to posses to a high degree.'

Widespread appeals, including one to the Home Secretary of the day, Sir George Grey, failed to save Baker. His execution at Winchester was witnessed by nearly 2000 people 'mostly of the working classes' according to the *Hampshire Advertiser*, 'who stood in solemn silence while the dreadful ceremony was being carried out.'

The song appeared as a broadside ballad. The tune has long been lost so we have added a tune which strives to keep as closely as possible to 'crime of passion' melodies.

The Southampton Tragedy

Within a gaol I am lamenting,
Will no one shed a tear for me;
In agony I'm sore relenting,
The author of a tragedy;
I dearly loved Naomi Kingswell,
But she alas proved false to me;
I in Southampton did her murder,
At the age of twenty-three.

Chorus
How could cursed Satan tempt me
To commit this tragedy,
And slay my lover in Southampton,
Aged scarcely twenty-three.

My sad name is Abraham Baker
I gazed on Naomi with delight
We were both reared up so tender,
In Newport, in the Isle of Wight:
Pleasant hours we passed together,
In sweet love and harmony;
Fondly I did love my Naomi,
And I thought she loved me.

In Southampton town we fellow-servants
Lived — how dreadful is my case
With the Rev. Mr. Poynder,
Number one in Moira Place;
My mind was always agitated,
Unless I could my Naomi see,
And oh! so fondly I did love her,
But Naomi did look cold on me.

I did prepare a fatal pistol,
And on the blessed Sabbath day
Determined I went to the kitchen
My own true love to kill and slay;
Suddenly I drew the trigger,
In Naomi's head I placed the ball,
My lover's death was instantaneous,
She on the kitchen floor did fall.

When the deed I had committed,
I did not attempt to flee —
Myself delivered up to justice, —
It was cursed jealousy
Caused me for to slay my lover —
Caused me for to take her life,
Because I thought my darling Naomi
Would refuse to be my wife.

Oh my father! Oh my mother!
Can you view the deed I've done,
And shed one single tear of sorrow
For your sad unhappy son
Who at the Bar must shortly answer
For the sad and dreadful deed?
You Southampton men and maidens
My confession closely read.

Read the fate of Abraham Baker, —
The Southampton Tragedy, —
Oh consider well and ponder,
Don't give way to jealousy;
That has caused my fatal ruin,
That did fill my mind with rage,
To slay and kill my own true lover
Abraham Baker did engage.

In the dark cells of Southampton,
A wretch I lie both day and night,
In the midst of youth and vigour
Scarcely reached the prime of life:
The deed I done now makes me shudder,
My guilty heart it wounds with pain,
Oh God! receive me in your mansion
To dwell with Naomi once again.

The Southampton Tragedy

Sprig of Thyme

This song, together with *The Seeds of Love*, are the archetypal English 'love' songs, though love is hardly the correct word in the case of this cautious song which warns maidens not to let any man steal their thyme. If *The Seeds of Love* is amorous dalliance from the man's point of view, *Sprig of Thyme* is the female counterbalance.

By and large, women do not fare very well in English folk song. This is not to say that English folk song is unfair to women: remember that folk song is only reflecting life around it. It is men's treatment of women which is at fault and folk song records the fact.

The secret code of lyrical folk song has many forms: in the industrial north, machines are used as emblems for various amorous functions; at sea nautical terms were substituted; and in the army, military terms meant the same thing. Thus 'digging in the mines', 'hand loom weaving', 'lowering tops'ls, top gans'ls and all', 'rap-a-tap-tap' (allegedly the sound of soldiers drilling), and other expressions all meant that sexual matters were getting serious. In other songs, the introduction of musical interludes ('I took out my fiddle and played her a tune') or elixirs ('This cordial that you talk about, there's very few that gets it') or animal pursuits ('I met a young maiden, her eyes like the sloes/Her teeth white as ivory and her cheeks like a rose/Her hair hung in ringlets on her shoulders so bare/And I said Pretty maid, have you seen my black hare?') — all these are more obvious metaphors; obvious to the country singer, at any rate, although the newcomer to folk song should not start looking for 'meanings' which are not there. The language of folk song is cunning and subtle.

The most common symbols used in folk song in the south of England are those used for sexual dalliance and intercourse. Most parts of the anatomy are emblemised in symbols, and in Hampshire most of these emblems take the form of flowers, plants and herbs. Thus the rose is love and the thorn is the pain of love or deceit; the lily and thyme are virginity, and so forth. With this in mind many songs which appear obscure will suddenly become quite clear: now we know what the singer means by 'I'll have you keep your gardens clean/And let no man steal your thyme'.

The version of *Sprig of Thyme* which we give here is a combined version of two taken down in 1906 by Gardiner in Basingstoke and Emery Down, in the New Forest. In our little book you will find several songs which have borrowed verses from other songs — 'floating verses' which drift from song to song. *Sprig of Thyme* borrows freely from its obvious companion, *The Seeds of Love*, so much so that one song leaves off to become almost the complete version of the other in a curious metamorphosis which is not unlike the change of caterpiller into butterfly. Such cross-breeding of songs can add interest to the lyric or the story, but it can create irritations for the singer when he hears a listener say halfway through a song — 'Oh, I know *this* bit!'

In the late 1980's a recording of the first part of this song became very popular; our version is substantially that published by Frank Purslow in *Marrow Bones* in 1965.

Sprig of Thyme

Come all you maidens fair,
That are just now in your prime,
I'll have you keep your gardens clean
And let no man steal your thyme.
    O once I had a sprig of thyme,
    And it flourished by night and by day,
    Till at length there came a false young man
    And he stole all my thyme away.
        So now my thyme is all gone,
        And I cannot plant any new,
        For the very place where my thyme used to grow
        Is all over-run with rue.
And rue is a running, running root
And it runs so far underneath
That I will pluck that running, running root
And I'll plant a jolly oak tree.
    Now here stands the jolly oak tree
    That will neither wither or die,
    And I'll prove so true to my dear love
    As the stars all in the sky.
        The gardener was standing by,
        I asked him to chose for me,
        He chose me the primrose, the violet and the vine,
        But I did them overlook all three.
In June there's the red rosy bud,
But that's not the flower for me,
For often times I've plucked at the red rosy bud
And gained the willow tree.
    Green willow it will twist,
    Green willow it will twine,
    I wish I was safe in that young man's arms
    That stole away my thyme.
        Green willow I will sing,
        Green willow shall be my song,
        That all the world may plainly see
        That I once loved a false young man.

Sprig of Thyme

The Stones of Eling Mill

Eling Tide Mill is, at the time of writing, the only working mill in England activated by the movements of the tide. And it is proving a great success into the bargain. How the mill works is this: twice a day the tides sweep up Southampton Water and into the Eling Channel beyond the mill. At full tide the sluice gates under the mill are closed, trapping the great mass of water in the channel. When the tide recedes, this trapped reservoir is released back through the sluices and on to an undershot water wheel which turns the stones in the mill.

The unique tidal system of the Solent region ensures a full capacity of head water which is never subject to water drought, nor does the mill rely on river water (which might dry up in a drought). And so the mill can be kept working at a full 8-hour capacity.

Flour produced by the mill, 100% stoneground, is sold on the premises and is eagerly bought up by health food shops and visitors to the mill. Having lain derelict for more than forty years the mill had been bought from Winchester College by the New Forest District Council and brought back to its former glory in a £50,000 restoration.

Ken Stephens is a Hampshire singer and songwriter who has penned many songs about local events and personalities, among them a ballad about the assassination of Lord Mountbatten whose home was at nearby Romsey. Ken's song about *The Stones of Eling Mill* has been recorded by *Forest Tracks*, the Hampshire-based recording company.

Eling Tide Mill — the only working tide mill in the world regularly producing wholemeal flour as it did centuries ago. The grinding stones are turned by releasing the harnessed power of the tides.

The Stones of Eling Mill

Verse 1 is also the chorus:

No sails to turn and no vanes to set,
For the waters are never still;
So bring your corn, we'll grind it to flour
'Twixt the stones of Eling Mill.

A ten-foot head in the mill dam's fine,
For the stones will run with a will,
And even when it's calm and fine
We're working at Eling Mill.

Chorus

When tower and post-mill come to a halt,
With no wind blowing over the hill,
The great big stones go merrily on
O'er the waters of Eling Mill.

Chorus

And as long as old Nature sends us the tides
We'll work away with a will,
And the gentry will come from far and wide
To trade at Eling Mill.

Chorus

The Stones of Eling Mill

Three Drunken Maidens

Here's a lovely Rabelaisean song from the Isle of Wight. Three buxom ladies, later joined by a fourth companion, show the lads how to enjoy a night out. We can almost see and hear the merriment, the splash of beer and the raucous laughter.

The song is quite unusual insofar as it shows women having a good time; more often than not women in folk songs are the victims of men's blandishments and cruelty, easily seduced and abandoned, and frequently — and quite literally — left holding the baby.

The song has turned up elsewhere and the late A.L. Lloyd recorded a version back in the 1960's. Largely through his recording the song filtered into the repertoires of new, younger folk singers and enjoyed a brief popularity in folk clubs, together with such flippant seduction songs as *The Gentleman Soldier* and *Queer Bungle Rye*. The time is ripe for a revival of the good-natured Island ladies' sprec.

A book of naughty songs called *Charming Phyllis's Garland* was published in the 1700's and a version of the *Drunken Maidens* appears within its covers.

The Island's notorious record of smuggling and ship-wrecking by hanging lights on the cliff-faces as a decoy to ships on stormy nights aids and abets the reputation of a community cocking a snoot at the law. Our four jolly girls, drinking and eating to excess, and straight out of Rowlandson, slip easily into the image.

Blackgang Chine, Isle of Wight. It was on the cliffs here that poachers and wreckers used to hang langerns on dark stormy nights to lure ships onto the rocks, thinking that they were steering towards a sheltered port.

Three Drunken Maidens

There were three drunken maidens
Came from the Isle of Wight,
They started drinking Saturday
Nor stopped till Sunday night;
When Sunday night came round, me boys,
They wouldn't then go out,
And them three drunken maidens
They pushed the glass about.

Then in came bouncing Sally
With her cheeks a rosy bloom,
'Move up, me jolly sisters,
And give young Sally some room.
For I'll be your equal
Before the night is out',
So now four drunken maidens
They pushed the glass about.

There was a woodcock and pheasant
And partridge and a hare,
And every sort of dainty,
No scarcity was there,
And forty pints of beer, me boys,
And still they wouldn't go out,
And them four drunken maidens
They pushed the glass about.

Then up came the old landlord
Asking for his pay,
And forty-pounds each, me boys,
Them girls was forced to pay;
They had forty-pounds a-piece, me boys,
And still they wouldn't go out,
But them four drunken maidens
They pushed the glass about.

Oh, where are your feather hats,
You maidens brisk and fine?
They've all been a-swallowed up
In tankards of good wine;
And where are your maidenheads,
You maidens brisk and gay?
We left them in the alehouse
For we've drunk them clean away!

Three Drunken Maidens

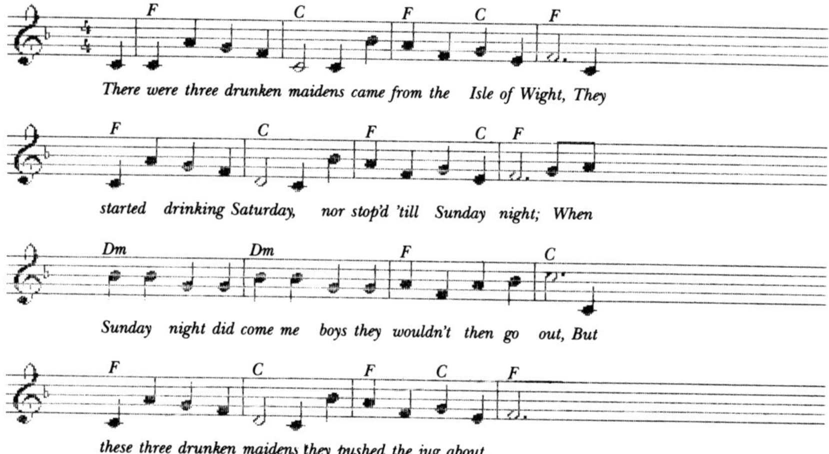

Whilst the Gamekeepers lie Sleeping

There are a handful of pubs in the New Forest where, over the heads of the day-tripper from the nearby towns and cities, the language turns on a sort of code. It goes beyond simple dialect and accent; and if one can learn to listen to this code and to understand it, a glimpse at life in the deep Forest may be obtained. The non-tourist activities of some of the inhabitants of the Forest are shrouded in this coded language, but to the initiated there are the stories of forays against gamekeepers, successes with bullet and hook and bow, as well as wire trap, against both man and beast. The townies' romantic image of the Forest poacher has little to do with the cruelty of some of the methods used to bring down a year-old prickett or snuff a terrified rabbit from its burrow.

Poaching may be a forbidden recreation of the New Forest but it is practiced on a wide scale nevertheless. Among the inhabitants of the New Forest who posses unusual skills in this occupation are the families of gypsies occupying encampments at places such as Shave Green — and less glamourously, housing estates at Bransgore and elsewhere. The artist and writer, Sven Berlin, has left us a vivid account of the life of some New Forest gypsies in his book *Dromengro — Man of the Road*. Without sacrificing his love for the gypsies, Berlin effectively dispels any illusion of the modern gypsy as a romantic figure.

English folk song is full of stories of poaching and some poaching songs are encoded seduction songs: this song is one such. In English folk song, a hare or rabbit is an emblem for a young woman, so you can imagine what the hunters or the poachers are about. These songs can be enjoyed on two levels — as straightforward gaming songs or as accounts of moonlit amorous engagements.

Whilst the Gamekeepers lie Sleeping was collected by George B. Gardiner from a resident of Marchwood in 1907. The following year it was also taken down from a 21-year old gypsy of Petersfield, not in itself a remarkable fact because the gypsies are fond of poaching songs. The repertoires of most gypsy families such as the Willetts of southern England and the Stewarts of Blairgowrie in Scotland contain a good percentage of these derring-do ballads.

The tune given here is the one noted by Frank Purslow in his excellent little book *Marrow Bones*, a collection drawn largely from the Gardiner and Hammond manuscripts.

Whilst the Gamekeepers lie Sleeping

I got a dog and a good dog too,
I keeps him in my keeping,
For to catch those hares that run by night
Whilst the gamekeepers lie sleeping.

My dog and me went out one night
For to learn some education,
Up jumps a hare and away she runs
Right into a large plantation.

She had not gone so very far
Before something stopped her running,
O aunt! O aunt! she loudly cried,
Stop a minute, your Uncle's coming!

Then I took out my old penknife
And quickly I did paunch her,
She turned out one of the female kind,
How glad am I I caught her.

I picked her up and I smoothed her down
And I put her in my keeping,
And I said to my dog It's time to be gone
Whilst the gamekeepers are still sleeping.

Away me and my dog did go,
Back into the town,
I took this hare to a labouring man
And I sold her for a crown.

We called into some public house,
And there we got quite mellow,
For we spent that crown and another one too,
Don't you think I'm a good-hearted fellow?

Whilst the Gamekeepers lie Sleeping

Winchester Gaol

Even today, the huge prison which stands on the brow of the hill overlooking the western side of Winchester is not a welcoming sight. The many unhappy associations don't help: it was here that Abraham Baker was hanged in 1856 for the murder of Naomi Kingswell; and another Baker — this time Frederick — was executed in 1867 for the murder of little Fanny Adams at Alton; and it was here, too, that the hapless heroine of Thomas Hardy's *Tess of the d'Urbervilles* ended her days on the prison's well-used gallows.

The area around the prison must have seen some horrendous sights, for we are told in old newspapers that the execution of Abraham Baker took place before a crowd of 2000 spectators — not an uncommon form of entertainment in the good old days. It was largely as a result of his correspondence with a national newspaper that Charles Dickens, who witnessed one such public spectacle and the revolting behaviour of the onlookers, was able to spearhead the movement which finally brought about the end of these open-air gatherings.

The prison was built in 1846 to replace the old Bridewell and Jewry Street gaol, and is a typical Victorian 'radial' prison with five wings of four storeys each, radiating out from a central tower. The gaol still serves a wayward clientele from Winchester and the surrounding area.

Charles Dickens, born in Portsmouth in 1812, witnessed a public execution and was so appalled by the behaviour of the onlookers that he conducted a campaign which helped bring about an end to these unpleasant spectacles.

Winchester saw its last execution in 1963. The last public execution in England was of James Searle in Stoke Abbot, Dorset, in 1858.

This little ballad was given to me by Bob Copper who, when he was landlord of the HH Inn at Cheriton, was one of the BBC's team of roving folk song collectors. He is also the head of the far-famed Copper family of Rottingdean in Sussex, retainers of some of the most evocative songs in the English tradition. Bob got the song from Victor Albert Spencer 'Turp' Brown of Cheriton, then a 70-year old wodsman. Turp was another man who carried a wealth of folk songs in his head and shortly before he died I was lucky enough to record him singing the mysterious *Streams of Lovely Nancy* at Bob Copper's old pub.

Winchester Gaol

There's a new county gaol in Winchester, Hants,
Where the young prosecutor is going to provance,
Because he'd no money, no friends to prevail,
Because he'd no money they sent him to gaol.

The turn-key came around the locks to unfold,
We stood there a-shivering and a-shaking with cold,
We stood there a-shivering and we couldn't get no rest
And we jumped out of bed almost starving to death.

The turn-key came around just twice in the day,
And bread and cold water was all he could say,
Just bread and cold water and you couldn't get enough,
Without any taste of the good liquor broth.

There's a new county gaol in Winchester, Hants,
Where the young prosecutor is going to provance,
And if you don't believe me and think this ain't true,
Just you go a-poaching and then you will know.

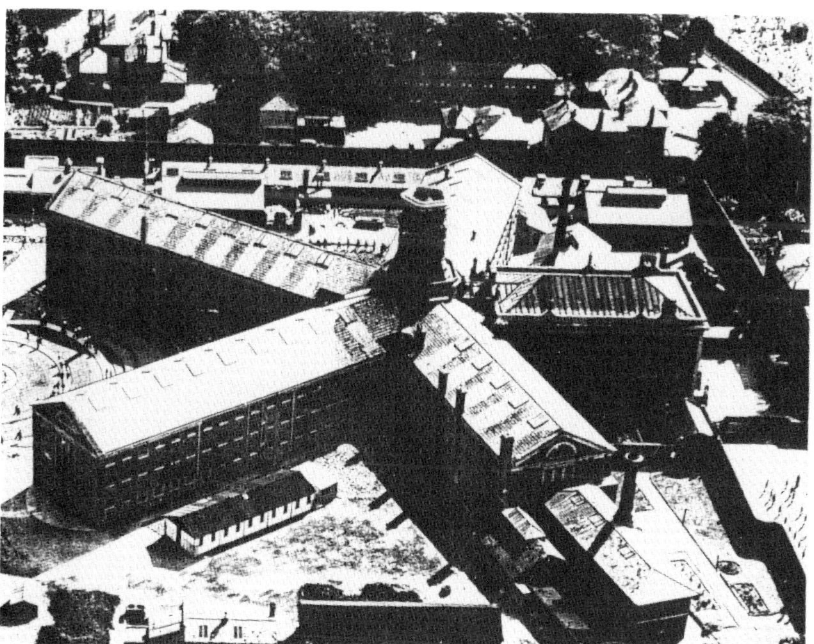

Winchester Goal: Tess of the d'Urbervilles may have been a fictional inmate, but Frederick and Abraham Baker were real enough.

Winchester Gaol

The Women of Leigh

'It's a warning to all young fellers to keep well aside from the girls of Leigh if they're lookin' for a bit of courtin'!'

So said the tiny old lady who gave me this song in 1960, underlining the cautionary advice of the song's last verse. Leigh is Eastleigh, and as she had lived there for most of her life, she reckoned she knew what she was talking about.

Personally, I've always found the women of Eastleigh to be every bit as charming as their sisters in the rest of the county, despite the grimness of some of the streets and the presence of yet another Pirelli's. The town has a lived-in look, enjoys a lively community spirit, and possesses a railway works so vast and dirt-covered that you would think that it must always have been there. Fact is, just a century ago the only buildings in the whole area were two smallholdings called Little Eastley and Great Eastley Farm.

The tune traditionally used for the song is well-known in various forms. If you listen carefully you can hear traces of a popular Norfolk folk song *Cruising Round Yarmouth*; and the Edwardian Irish songwriter, Percy French, used it for his *Emigrant's Letter* — sometimes known as *Cutting the Corn in Creeslough*.

Our chorus, 'Damn, damn' etc, is a corruption of the usual 'Down, down, down derry down'.

James Reeves, the poet and children's writer, said in his study of English folk song *The Idiom of the People*: 'The refrain 'derry down' seems to be connected with an obscene dance mentioned by Dunbar in *Ane Brash of Wowing*':

Syne tha till ane play began,
Quhilk that thay call the dirrydan.

The Women of Leigh

Come all you young lovers and listen to me,
A warning I'm giving as clearly you'll see,
Concerning the woman I thought was my own,
She's gone with some other and left me alone.

Chorus
Singing Damn, damn, rigmarole damn,
I thought that she loved me but she let me down.

I wandered one evening to see my true love,
The moon and the stars were shining above;
She called me her lover, she called me her man,
But that was the last that I saw of my Jan.

Chorus

I strayed to her cottage but found she had gone,
I thought of her sadly as I went along;
I thought of the lies that she plied upon me,
And I bitterly thought of her inconstancy.

Chorus

So all you young lovers take warning by me,
Have nothing to do with the women of Leigh;
They'll treat you to pleasure and call you their own,
But then in the morning you'll find they have gone.

Chorus

The Women of Leigh

The Woolston Ferry

Michael Sadler, who wrote this song, used to call it a 'land shanty': it poked a little bit of fun at the heroics of the sea shanty of the commercial clipper ships of the 1800's. At the same time, his song follows a time-honoured process of enshrining in heroic style those little details of everyday life which tends to pass unnoticed under our gaze. How many of us who used to queue in the rain waiting for the floating bridge to clank its way across the Itchen towards us ever thought of its being worthy of a song, even a comic song? How many of us who cursed its irregular time-keeping as we stood wet and cold, already late for work, ever thought that one day we would mourn its passing?

A ferry had crossed the Itchen for many generations, linking the town of Southampton with Woolston, its suburb 'across the sea', before the first 'floating bridge' went into operation in 1833. In those days the Itchen was a serious barrier between Southampton and the eastern side of the county and the Itchen Bridge Company was created to profit from travellers wishing to journey to Portsmouth and beyond. Even before this time a fixed bridge had been envisaged which would link the town side's Crosshouse with the far side's Itchen Village, but the floating bridge was the logical expedient. And so it remained until 1977 when the last of the ferries gave way to the finally realised Itchen Bridge.

Mike Sadler's song recalls many of the eccentricities of floating bridge travel. He wrote the words and set them to an American tune called *The Midnight Special* but added a shade of complexity to the opening lines by setting them to a negro spiritual, *Swing Low, Sweet Chariot*. An Irish song called *The Buncrana Train* dwells on the same sort of parochial details which gives Sadler's song its charm. *The Woolston Ferry* surprised the pundits by becoming a best-selling record at the time of the closure of the old bridge.

Incidentally, in 1415 two conspirators against King Henry V — then amassing his armies at Southampton in preparation for departure to France — tried to escape by crossing the Itchen at the place where the floating bridge was eventually to cross. They were apprehended on the Woolston side, brought back to trial in Southampton (some say the trial took place in the High Street's *Red Lion* pub, though there is no documentary evidence for this), and executed at the Bargate.

(See my notes on *The Ship in Distress*.)

The Woolston Ferry

(First verse sung to the well-known spiritual *Swing Low, Sweet Chariot*):

I looked over Woolston and what did I see
Coming for to carry me home?
That old Woolston Ferry coming towards me,
Coming for to carry me home.

(Remaining verses and choruses to the tune of
The Midnight Special).

If you're ever up in Sholing
And you want to go to town,
Don't go by Bitterne
—That's the long way round.
  Take a trip across the ferry,
  Take a trip across the sea,
  And if you're a pedestrian
  You can go for free.

Chorus
On the Woolston Ferry,
It doesn't travel very fast,
It was never built for comfort,
It was built to last.

On two steel hawsers
Across the river it will creep,
The steel glints in the sunlight
And flops back into the deep.
  And from the deck of the ferry
  —What a wonderful sight:
  They shipwrights grafting
  At Thorneycroft's on the right.

Chorus

Go and see Lowry's painting
In the Art Gallery,
Of this wonderful relic
Of a past century;
  And when I speak of its construction
  You'll be surprised to learn
  That the bow going one way
  Coming back becomes the stern.

See the weather-beaten captain
With his weather-beaten tan,
He don't wear no gold braid
    —He's a corporation man.
    But the captains of the ferry
    They're a dying race,
    There are no ex-tram drivers
    To take their place.

Chorus

But the floating bridge has had it,
It will have to go,
The motorists don't like it,
Sixteen p. a throw;
    So they built a bridge of concrete,
    Very modern, very high,
    Every time I use it
    I look down and heave a sigh.

Chorus

The Floating Bridge, Southampton by L.S. Lowry.
(Courtesy, Southampton City Art Gallery)

The Woolston Ferry

The Young Sailor Cut Down in his Prime

This is one of the most widespread of all English folk songs. Its pedigree is not particularly noble (any more than its sentiments), but it has left its mark on the traditions of several countries.

It used to be an Irish song called *The Unfortunate Rake*. This overlapped with a jazz version called *St James's Infirmary*, sometimes *The St James' Infirmary Blues*. It became a New Orleans ballad called *Gambler's Blues* and went out west in the 1860's where it was found by John Lomax, the famous American folk song collector, among cowboys who sang it as *The Streets of Laredo*:

> As I went out in the streets of Lardeo,
> As I walked out in Laredo one day,
> Who should I meet but one of my comrades
> All wrapped in white linen and cold as the clay...

In this version the hero, a gambler, has been shot for being a bad loser in a card game. The British versions have central figures who are either soldier or sailor, and are less romantic than the cowboy. The mention of 'pills of white mercury' reveals that the unfortunate hero has perished of an unmentionable but well-known social disease. There is a rueful irony in his last request: 'six pretty fair maids to carry white roses' to disguise the stench from his rotting corpse.

The Royal Albion, named in several versions of the song, must be the most famous pub in English folk song and, although it no longer stands, has brought old Portsmouth a certain unsavoury celebrity.

The version given here mixes two fragments of the song in a bizarre cocktail: at the beginning of the song our lamented sailor is being buried at sea, and yet in verse 4 we are being told of his gravestone...

The Young Sailor Cut Down in his Prime

As I was a-walking down by the Royal Albion,
Cold was the morning and dark was the day,
Who should I meet with but one of my mess-mates
All wrapped in white linen and colder than clay.

Refrain
So beat the drum slowly and play the fife merrily,
Play the dead march as you carry me on,
And over the side as you lower my coffin
Say There's a young sailor cut down in his prime.

Get six of my mess-mates to carry my coffin,
Six of my mess-mates to carry me high,
And six pretty fair maids to carry white roses
So the people won't smell me as I pass them by.

Now had she but told me before she had ruined me,
Had she but warned me all in a good time,
I might have a-taken those pills of white mercury,
But now I'm a sailor cut down in my prime.

On a stone at his grave you will see these words written:
Now all you young sailors take warning by me,
And don't go a-courting flash girls of the city,
Flash girls of the city have been the ruin of me.

The Young Sailor Cut Down in his Prime

Selected Bibliography

Books on folk songs and books *of* folk songs are numerous enough to fill libraries and the most accessible collection of such books in this country is the Vaughan Williams Memorial Library at Cecil Sharp House, home of the English Folk Dance and Song Society, London. The manuscript collection of George B. Gardiner's Hampshire songs is housed here.

The following selective list only concerns the songs covered by this book together with a skeleton study of the folk songs of Britain which will help the reader who wishes to do so place the songs of Hampshire in their wider context.

Ashton, J. *Real Sailor Songs.* Leadenhall Press 1891. (reprinted by The Broadsheet King, 1973)

Bell, Robert. *Ancient Poems, Ballads and Songs of the Peasantry of England.* Parker 1857.

Bronson, Bertrand H. *The Traditional Tunes of the Child Ballads.* Princetown University Press, USA 1959—66.

Chappell, William. *Popular Music of the Olden Time,* 2 volumes. Chappell 1883.

Child, Francis J. *The English and Scottish Popular Ballads,* 5 volumes 1882—98.

Copper, Bob. *Songs and Southern Breezes.* Heinemann 1973.

Dean Smith, Margaret. *A Guide to English Folk Song Collections 1822 —1952.* Liverpool University Press 1954.

Firth, C.H. *Naval Songs and Ballads.* Navy Records Society 1908.

Gardiner, George B. *Folk Songs of Hampshire.* Novello 1909.

Helm, Alex. *5 Mumming Plays for Schools.* EFDSS/The Folk-lore Society 1965.

Hugill, Stan. *Shanties from the Seven Sea.* Routledge & Kegan Paul 1961.

Journal of the Folk-song Society. Vol III No 13, 1909.

Lloyd, A.L. *The Singing Englishman.* Workers' Music Association 1944.

Lloyd, A.L. *Folk Song in England.* Lawrence and Wishart 1967.

Long, W.H. *Dialect of the Isle of Wight.* Reeves & Turner 1886.

Palmer, Roy. *A Touch on the Times.* Penguin 1974.

Palmer, Roy. *The Rambling Soldier.* Penguin 1977.

Palmer, Roy. *The Valiant Sailor.* Cambridge University Press 1973.

Purslow, Frank. *Marrow Bones.* EFDS Publications 1965.

Purslow, Frank. *The Constant Lovers.* EFDS Publications 1972.

Reeves, James. *The Idiom of the People.* Heinemann 1958.

Sharp, Cecil J. *English Folk Song: Some Conclusions* Simpkin and Novello 1907, (reprinted Mercury Books 1965).

Shepard, Leslie. *The Broadside Ballad.* Herbert Jenkins 1962.

Shepard, Leslie. *History of Street Literature.* David & Charles 1973.

Simpson, Claude M. *The British Broadside Ballad and its Music.* Rutgers University Press, USA 1966.

Smith, G.B. *Illustrated British Ballads,* 2 volumes. Cassells 1881.

The Author

JOHN PADDY BROWNE was born in Derry City, Northern Ireland in 1939 but has lived in Hampshire for the past 30 years. He gave his first talk on folk song while still at school and since then has lectured all over Britain and in Europe including a series of talks in Eastern Bloc countries. He has written extensively on folk song and most of the other arts in several hundred essays, many of which have appeared in foreign language translations. He has contributed to several books on folk song, history and art, and one of his own books *Selected Poems* has been published this year.

He has also appeared on television and broadcast on many radio stations, usually on the subject of folk music. His collection of traditional songs, gathered at first hand from farm workers, itinerant singers, mine workers and ethnic groups, has been used on radio, record and in concert by some of the country's professional singers.

A cartographer by profession, he publishes reproductions of old maps under his own logo *The Sign of the Star* and is the editor of a folk music magazine.

His book *Folk Songs of Old Hampshire* is the first book to deal comprehensively with the traditional and contemporary songs of this county.